Mary of Gueldres

Mary
m.
James, 1st Lord Hamilton

...ry

...uvergne

...bany

Elizabeth
m.
Matthew Stewart
2nd Earl of Lennox

James, 1st Earl of Arran

John Stewart
3rd Earl of Lennox
d. 1526

Sir James
Hamilton
of Finnart

James, 2nd Earl of Arran
Duke of Châtelhérault

...argaret m. Matthew Stewart
...las 4th Earl of Lennox

JAMES V

KING OF SCOTS

by the same author

THE MAKING OF A KING

James V and Madeleine of France from the Seton Armorial

James the fyſt
began his Raÿn
1514 He maryed firſt
Maȝdelena dorhter
of francis ye fwrſt
k of france

JAMES V

KING OF SCOTS
1512-1542

Caroline Bingham

COLLINS
ST JAMES'S PLACE, LONDON
1971

William Collins Sons & Co Ltd
London · Glasgow · Sydney · Auckland
Toronto · Johannesburg

First published 1971
© Caroline Bingham 1971
ISBN 0 00 211390 2
Set in Monotype Caslon
Made and Printed in Great Britain by
William Collins Sons & Co Ltd Glasgow

FOR
ANDREW

Contents

List of Illustrations

Acknowledgements

I would like to express my gratitude to Major Michael Crichton Stuart of Falkland for kindly allowing me to see the portrait of James V and Marie de Guise at Falkland Palace, and for his permission to reproduce the picture as an illustration to this book. I am equally grateful to Sir David Ogilvy Bt., for kindly allowing me to reproduce two pictures from the Seton Armorial. I would also like to thank Dr Rae of the National Library of Scotland, Dr Anne Robertson of the Hunterian Museum, and Dr Duncan Thomson of the Scottish National Portrait Gallery for their help in the matter of illustrations.

I am very grateful to Mr Iain Stuart Robertson for lending me a typescript of his forthcoming book *An Introduction to the Poetry of Scotland* and for allowing me to quote from it. And I would like to thank Mr Norman Lothian, Chief Guide at Falkland, for sparing his time to discuss with me the traditional anecdotes of James V, and for lending me several books.

Finally, I am especially grateful to Mr Richard Ollard of Collins, a most sympathetic editor; to my parents, Cedric and Muriel Worsdell, who have given me so much encouragement; and to my daughter, Frances Bingham, who has shown a great deal of patience with that rather abstracted type of being, a parent who is writing a book.

AUTHOR'S NOTE

In order to prevent the reader being faced with frequent passages of unfamiliar language I have translated quotations from sixteenth century Scots prose sources into modern English. In quoting sixteenth century Scots poetry, however, I have attempted to retain the flavour of the original forms by merely anglicizing the spelling, and by leaving unaltered words which affect the rhyme schemes. A glossary of these words is provided at the foot of the page on which they occur.

Chapter One

KING AND COUNTRY

'If he had received good counsel of wise and godly men . . . he had been the most noblest Prince that ever reigned in the realm of Scotland.'

Lindsay of Pitscottie

'So sore a dread King and so ill beloved of his subjects was never in this land . . .'

Norfolk to Thomas Cromwell
15th September, 1537

KING JAMES V of Scotland, the nephew of Henry VIII of England and the father of Mary, Queen of Scots, reigned for twenty-nine years and three months. For fourteen of those years he ruled his kingdom autocratically and until near the end with apparent success; yet his reign ended in failure and he died in tragic circumstances at the age of thirty, after the defeat of his army by the English at Solway Moss, in 1542.

James V was the last Catholic King of a Catholic Scotland. Possibly he was fortunate in dying before his kingdom was torn in two by the great conflict of the Reformation, a conflict which exhausted the energy and wore out the spirit of his widow, the Queen-Regent Marie de Guise, and contributed in great part to the downfall of their daughter, Mary Queen of Scots.

To the historians of the immediately ensuing generation, James V did not appear as controversial a figure as either his widow or his daughter. They, personally involved in the events of the Reformation and the immediate post-Reformation period, were inevitably praised by the Catholic and vilified by the Protestant historians. James V, who had quitted the scene before the outbreak of the conflict which aroused such violent antagonisms, could be viewed somewhat more impartially. On the whole, from the historians of both parties, he received a good press.

Of three historians who were his late contemporaries it was inevitable that the Catholic Bishop Lesley would be the most laudatory. The Protestant scholar and historian George Buchanan tempered his praise with reservations. He praised the King's attainments, acknowledged his virtues, and, as befitted an educationalist, blamed his shortcomings on an inadequate education and an undisciplined upbringing. The Protestant chronicler Lindsay of Pitscottie declared that if James V "had received good counsel of wise and godly men, and had left the evil counsel of his papist bishops, he had been the noblest Prince that ever reigned in the realm of Scotland."[1]

The reputation of James V continued to rise, and when the poet William Drummond of Hawthornden wrote his *History of Scotland* in the seventeenth century he crowned the earlier writers' praises of James V with a graceful eulogy:

"All his faults are but some few warts in a most pleasing and beautiful face. He was much beholding to the excellent poets of his time whose commendation shall serve him for an epitaph." The commendations which Drummond quoted were by Ariosto, who knew the King only by report, and Ronsard, who was personally acquainted with him. According to the former, James was

Di vertu esempio et di bellezza raro.*

According to the latter:

Son port estoit royal, son regard vigoureux
De vertus, et d'honneur, et de guerre amoureux
La douceur et la force illustroient son visage
Si que Vénus et Mars en avoient fait partage.[2]

* i.e. of unexampled virtue and beauty rare.

The historians of the ensuing centuries, though less influenced by the compliments which the excellent poets of James's time had offered him, continued to judge him favourably until, at the end of the nineteenth century P. Hume Brown, whose *History of Scotland* long remained a standard work, assumed a more critical tone:

"The course and conclusion of James's reign are the sufficient comment on his capacity as a ruler . . . The state in which James V left his kingdom . . . seems the sufficient proof that he did not possess the administrative capacity of his father."[3]

That James V was merely a less able King than his father James IV remained the generally accepted view of him, until a distinguished Scottish historian of the present century, Professor Gordon Donaldson, wrote an outspoken condemnation of both his character and his rule:

"The vindictiveness which made his later years something of a reign of terror went so far beyond what was politic that it suggests a streak of sadistic cruelty in his nature . . . He was, after all, half a Tudor by birth and perhaps a Tudor rather than a Stewart in character. He combined in his own person the acquisitiveness of his grandfather, Henry VII, the lust and ruthlessness of his uncle, Henry VIII, and the unrelenting cruelty of his cousin, Bloody Mary."[4]

The reputations of kings inevitably undergo changes as history is rethought and rewritten by successive generations. But, if the same man can inspire such diverse judgments as those passed on James V (and judgments are based not only on the information available at the time of writing, or on changing views of what is praiseworthy, but also on the personal feelings of the writer) then it seems likely that the truth about that man will prove to be more complex than either his eulogists or his critics would have their readers believe. The purpose of this book is to attempt, from the diversity of contemporary and later judgments, as true a portrayal as possible of James V, both as an individual and as a King of Scots.

It is by returning to the writings of a late contemporary of James V that the reader comes upon the most convincing glimpse of James as a complex and inconsistent individual. The Reformer John Knox, when he assumed the role of historian, was not always as judicious in summing up character as he appears in the following sketch of James V:

"He was called by some a good poor man's king; of others he was termed a murderer of the nobility, and one that had decreed their whole destruction. Some praised him for the repressing of theft and oppression; others dispraised him for the defouling of men's wives, and virgins. And thus men spoke even as their affections led them. And yet none spoke altogether beside the truth; for a part of all these foresaid were so manifest that as the virtues could not be denied, so could not the vices by any craft be cloaked."[5]

What it meant to be a King of Scots may be best explained by some account of the country itself.

*   *   *

Scotland, the northernmost portion of the island which contains the three countries of Scotland, England and Wales, has a total area of only about 30,000 square miles. The 787 islands, which are scattered mostly along the west coast and to the north, make up just over one tenth of the whole.

The Western Isles became subject to the Crown of Scots in the thirteenth century, in the reign of Alexander III. But from the middle of the fourteenth to the end of the sixteenth century, under a series of chiefs of the clan Donald, who styled themselves Lords of the Isles, the Western Isles maintained an existence virtually independent of Scotland. James IV had some success in integrating the Isles into his kingdom, but the independence of island chiefs could still be a threat in the reign of James V.

The archipelagoes of Orkney and Shetland, which lie

to the north of Scotland, were the last acquisition of the Crown of Scots. They came under Scottish rule when James III received the royal estates of the Danish Crown in Orkney and Shetland in lieu of the dowry of his bride, Margaret of Denmark, in 1469. Orcadians and Shetlanders still remain strongly aware of their Scandinavian inheritance, and of basic differences between themselves and the mainland Scots.

The mainland of Scotland is divided into Highlands and Lowlands, terms which are only relative since the Lowlands contain some land that is wild and mountainous and the Highlands some that is flat and fertile. On the whole, however, the mountain masses of the Highlands are higher and more impenetrable and the agricultural land of the Lowlands more fertile and much greater in extent. The division of the Highlands and the Lowlands is not a lateral division of the country into its northern and southern halves. The "Highland Line" is a wavering division which runs down the mainland from about the centre of the northern coastline southwestwards almost, but not quite, to the extreme southwest of the country. South-east of this diagonal is Lowland; north-west of it, Highland. Therefore the whole of the eastern seaboard, all the way from Caithness to Berwick, is Lowland, and the Lowlands take in Galloway in the Southwest.

The Border, the frontier of Scotland and England, was not decided by geography but by history. Much fought over and many times altered, it is an irrational boundary. Thus, Berwickshire is a Scottish county, but the town of Berwick, lost to the Crown of Scots in 1482, is in England.

The Borderers of Scotland and northern England – despite centuries spent in fighting one another – have much in common, but within Scotland the division into Highland and Lowland, is not only geographical but ethnological. The Highland Scots are Celts, and in the sixteenth century they were Gaelic speaking; there are Gaelic speakers in the

Highlands and Western Isles still, but except in some of the
Isles they are now a minority. The Lowland Scots of the
sixteenth century spoke Scots, not Scottish-accented English,
and a Spanish ambassador to Scotland, Pedro de Ayala,
explained in his reports that the Scots and English languages
were as different from each other as Aragonese and Castilian
Spanish.

The Lowland Scots, of Saxon stock with admixtures
of Norman and, especially in the north-east, of Scandinavian
blood, were keenly aware of the racial and linguistic difference between the Highland Scots and themselves, and they
considered themselves a great deal more civilized. The
economy of the Lowlands was based on agriculture,
fishing and maritime trade. Wine, and most luxury goods
were imported. The principal exports, according to Æneas
Sylvius Piccolomini (later Pope Pius II) who visited James I
in 1435, were hides, wool, salted fish and pearls. The Lowlands contained the principal cities: Edinburgh, St Andrews,
Perth, Dundee and Aberdeen; both the Archbishoprics:
Glasgow and St Andrews; and all three Universities:
Glasgow, Aberdeen and St Andrews. In the Lowlands
also were almost all the larger ecclesiastical foundations,
and all the royal residences.

In the Highlands there was still a pastoral economy,
for the Celts did not take readily to the building of towns,
or to the urban life and trade that had developed in the
Lowlands, and much of the land was unsuitable for agriculture.

The Lowland Scots regarded the Celts and their way of
life as savage. John Major, writing in the reign of James V,
described the Lowlanders as "householding Scots", and
the Highlanders he designated the "Wild Scots". He wrote
of them as follows:

"In dress, in the manner of their outward life, and in good
morals, for example, these come behind the householding
Scots . . . One part of the Wild Scots have a wealth of cattle,

James IV from the Seton Armorial

Margaret Tudor by Daniel Mytens, after an original portrait, artist unknown

sheep and horses . . . The other part of these people delight in the chase and a life of indolence . . . They are full of mutual dissensions, and war rather than peace is their normal condition . . . Our householding Scots . . . these men hate, on account of their differing speech, as much as they do the English".[6]

The differences between Highlanders and Lowlanders, racial, linguistic and economic, were further emphasized by difference in dress. The Lowlanders were influenced by European fashion. James V is portrayed wearing clothes of similar styles to those of Henry VIII of England, François Ier of France and the Emperor Charles V, the European sovereigns who were his contemporaries. The nobility, the lairds and the urban middle class would have copied him in style, the materials of the clothes providing the measure of the wearer's social status. A satirical poem by Sir David Lindsay of the Mount makes it clear that country girls copied the dress of court ladies. In his *Contemptioun of Syde Taillis* he mocks the wearers of impractical sweeping skirts which dragged through the mud and ordure of farmyards. The Highlanders were not influenced by European fashion. As Major described them:

"From the mid-leg to the foot they go uncovered; their dress is, for an over garment, a loose plaid, and a shirt saffron-dyed. They are armed with bow and arrows, a broadsword and a small halbert. They always carry in their belt a stout dagger, single-edged but of the sharpest. In time of war they cover the whole body with a coat of mail, made of iron rings, and in it they fight. The common people among the wild Scots go out to battle with the whole body clad in a linen garment sewed together in patchwork, well daubed with wax or with pitch, and with an over-coat of deer-skin".[7]

While it is necessary to stress the basic differences and the visible contrasts between the Highland and Lowland Scots, it is also important to notice the characteristics which they had in common. Both, according to Major, shared the characteristic of extreme bellicosity, "If two nobles of equal rank happen to be very near neighbours" he wrote "quarrels and even shedding of blood are a common thing between them; and their very retainers cannot meet without strife..." Their habits were copied by those of lower status: "The farmers . . . keep a horse and weapons of war, and are ready to take part in his quarrel, be it just or unjust, with any powerful lord, if they only have a liking for him, and with him, if need be, to fight to the death . . . they therefore bring up their children to take service with the great nobles . . ."[8]

In the matter of local loyalties there was considerable similarity between the Highland and Lowland Scots. In the Highlands geographical barriers encouraged localism. In each locality the local unit was the clan, in theory an extension of the family (The Gaelic word for children is "clann") and loyalty was owed, on the basis of theoretical blood relationship, to the chief. Loyalty to the clan in the Highlands was paralleled by loyalty to the "name" in the Lowlands. Thus, the Douglas Earls of Angus would claim the loyalty of all those of the name of Douglas, and the Hamilton Earls of Arran would have a similar claim over all those of the name of Hamilton. The link between the chief and those of his name was very close. When, in the reign of James V, the Earl of Angus was exiled, the Douglases *en bloc* fell from favour and lost their possessions with him. It would be an over simplification to describe the structure of society as 'tribal' in the Highlands and 'feudal' in the Lowlands. A feudal structure of land tenure existed in the Highlands, and lowlanders' loyalty to the name could be fairly described as tribal.

Besides sharing certain social characteristics, the Highlands and the Lowlands shared three institutions which could have been expected to exert a unifying influence: the law, the Church and the monarchy.

The law was less effective as a unifying influence than might have been expected, for although the laws applied universally throughout the country, the legal system worked very largely through local administration. The Law therefore could serve as much to strengthen local influences as to dispense nationwide royal justice. For instance, technically a local magnate might be a royal official, but if he possessed a heritable jurisdiction, its powers conferred upon him a considerable degree of independence from the Crown and his local prestige served to enhance his legal powers. If he possessed a charter of "regality" he would have "a system of legal administration reproducing in miniature that of the Kingdom",[9] and his courts would probably have the competence to try all cases except those involving treason. Except under the rule of a very strong king the legal system was in danger of developing the abuses attendant upon local influence and its inevitable concomitant of private interest.

Similar considerations applied, though less strongly, to the Church. Like the laws, the Catholic religion was common to the whole country. But the higher clergy came mostly from the noble families. For instance, the poet Gavin Douglas, Bishop of Dunkeld, was the third son of the fifth Earl of Angus. Certain benefices came to be regarded as the perquisites of particular families. Local influence could make itself felt through the authority of the Church and the Ecclesiastical Courts as well as through the secular courts. Nevertheless, the Crown had great influence over the Church, particularly after 1487 when Pope Sixtus IV granted to the King of Scots the privilege of having his nominations to major benefices considered at Rome. In practice the Kings of Scots thereafter had effective powers of nomination. There was a tendency, when the King was on bad terms with his nobility, for him to make an ally of the Church through the party of his own nominees. The reliance of James V on "his papist bishops" under these circumstances did the Church little good as the Reformation approached. In both local and national influence the Church steadily lost ground during the reign of James V.

Potentially the most effective unifying influence upon Scotland was the monarchy. As an institution the monarchy possessed great prestige. The King was the symbol and the embodiment of the nation's identity and the independence which it had fought hard and long to maintain against the territorial ambitions of the Kings of England. The first of the Stewarts was accounted the hundredth King from the legendary, or perhaps mythical, King Fergus. The legendary antiquity of the monarchy greatly supported the prestige of the King, and if the histories of Fergus and his early successors as recorded by Hector Boece and George Buchanan are now as lightly regarded as Geoffrey of Monmouth's stories of the early Kings of Britain, it must be remembered that in the sixteenth century they were wholeheartedly believed.

The man who enjoyed the prestige of being the hundredth King of Scots was Robert II, who succeeded in 1371. He was the son of Walter, sixth hereditary High Steward of Scotland (hence the surname of Stewart) and the Princess Margery, daughter of King Robert the Bruce. When David II, the son of Robert the Bruce, died without heirs, the succession was settled by statute upon the descendants of Margery and her husband. Thereafter the Stewarts were fortunate in that there were no further succession crises; the succession continued from father to son in unbroken primogeniture until James V died leaving a daughter, Mary Queen of Scots, who was unquestioningly accepted as the sovereign.

In other respects the Stewarts were not so fortunate. Monarchy is an institution which for its efficaciousness relies very greatly upon the character of the individual King. Strong kings create a strong monarchy but the institution is weakened by the rule of ineffectual kings and by minorities. The Stewart dynasty began with two elderly, ailing kings, Robert II and Robert III, and the death of the latter was followed by nineteen years of ineffectual regency, while the young King James I, captured by the English at the age of eleven, remained a prisoner in England until he was thirty. He returned to Scotland to find a country in which there was a complete absence of law and order, and in which the strongest loyalties were given to the great lords who had gained in power and independence during years of ineffectual rule. James I was largely successful in his vow to "make the key keep the castle and the bracken bush the cow", and in making himself respected and obeyed as no king had been since Robert the Bruce. But though he was popular with the commons his disciplining of the nobility aroused sufficient antagonism to lead to his murder in 1437, and his successes remained unconsolidated.

A struggle for power between the Crown and its overmighty subjects was the principal theme of fifteenth century politics in both Scotland and England, but in Scotland the struggle derived its particular pattern from the series of minorities which prevented each King from building upon the achievements of his predecessor. On the death of James I his heir was a child of six. Like his father, James II found the ambitions of his nobility his greatest problem, especially the overweening ambition of the house of Douglas. He was a warlike and vigorous King who set about reducing his nobility to obedience by force of arms. But his career came to a premature and tragic end when he was killed accidentally in 1460, at the age of thirty. He was succeeded by his eight year old son, James III, who was doubly unfortunate in facing the same problem as his father and grandfather all over again and in being more interested in the arts than in war or government. James III antagonized a dangerously large proportion of his nobility who rebelled against him in the name of his son. He was murdered in 1488. James IV, fortunately for himself and for Scotland, succeeded at the relatively mature age of fifteen.

It is possible to overpaint the picture of the disorder which occurred during the minorities of the Stewart Kings, but undoubtedly each minority caused a setback to the power of the monarchy, and each King had a struggle to assert himself against those nobles who had been in power during his minority before he himself could begin to rule. But in spite of the setbacks, the monarchy had gradually gained in prestige and power. James IV, popular and successful, might have left his son a kingdom in which many of the perennial problems were well on the way to solution; it was external events which brought about disaster, and resulted in the accession of an infant in whose minority the same situation would arise as had faced his predecessors.

James IV endeavoured, as the preceding Kings had done, to increase the rule of law, and beyond that he sought to improve the quality of the justice that was administered both in the King's courts and under local jurisdictions. He endeavoured not only to discipline his lords but to win their support, in which he was more successful than any of his predecessors. He was aware, as apparently none of his predecessors had been, of the importance not only of keeping order in the Highlands and the Isles, but of integrating them into his Kingdom. He alone of the Stewart Kings spoke Gaelic, which was a great assistance to him in winning the trust of the Highland Scots. He did not reign long enough to integrate the disparate elements of his kingdom as he desired, but at least he won the personal loyalty of many of the Highland Chiefs, an achievement upon which much might have been built. Unfortunately his achievement was brought to an end by events which were beyond his control.

Since the time of James I Scotland had been fortunate in that the long minority of Henry VI of England and the turmoil of the War of the Roses had prevented the English

Crown from pursuing the traditional policy of the Plantagenets of attempting the conquest of Scotland. Edward IV
had been strong enough to meddle in Scottish affairs, and
his support of James III's treacherous brother, Alexander,
Duke of Albany, had occasioned the loss of Berwick. But
the uneasy reign of Richard III and the early years of the
Tudor dynasty had marked a period of better relations
between the two countries. An English alliance had been
the unpopular policy of James III, and Henry VII of
England, the ally of that king's last years, had offered a
continuance of the same policy and had married his elder
daughter, Margaret, to James IV, in 1503. With the accession of Henry VIII, however, the Tudor dynasty was
sufficiently firmly established for the traditional attitude of
English Kings towards Scotland to reassert itself. Henry
VIII succeeded in 1509, and by 1512 his inimical behaviour
towards his brother-in-law James IV had forced Scotland
to renew the traditional "auld alliance" with France.

The auld alliance, like the monarchy, had a legendary
antiquity, but in fact its formal beginning was in 1295,
and thereafter it was renewed many times. France had
benefited from Scottish assistance against the English
in the Hundred Years War, and indeed had demonstrably
received help more often than rendered it. But the alliance
had not been entirely unequal, for if France had received
more political and military benefit, for Scotland the benefit
of the alliance had been cultural, it had served "to plant
some lilies in the 'cauld kail-yaird'."[10]

In 1512, France, involved in the Italian wars, was
threatened by a 'Holy League' between the Papacy, Venice,
Spain and England. The following year Henry VIII invaded France in pursuit of military glory, which he attained
by winning a pointless but showy victory at Guinegate.
France appealed to James IV to honour the auld alliance by
administering to England a thrust in the back which should
make King Henry pay dearly for his gains in France. The

response to this appeal was the disastrous prelude to the reign of James V.

* * *

On 22nd August 1513 James IV invaded England, and on the night of 8th September his army of about twenty thousand men was encamped in Northumberland, on Flodden Edge. That army was a remarkable illustration of the universal support that James IV had won, for the greatest of the nobility, the leading churchmen, the Highland Chiefs, the lesser lords and the lairds had all brought their contingents. In after years the Scots were to complain that they had been led into a war on behalf of an ally who showed little gratitude for the sacrifice they made. But at the time they readily followed a popular King against the "auld enemy."

James IV has often been blamed for being anachronistically chivalrous, and needlessly allowing himself to be out-generalled at Flodden by the Earl of Surrey, the commander of the army which Henry VIII had left to defend the north of England. According to the Spanish ambassador, Pedro de Ayala, James IV's principal fault as a general was that "he begins to fight even before he has given his orders". But in what Ayala criticized as impetuousness, James IV had a quality of leadership appreciated by the soldiery of Scotland. In 1513 he was a figure from the past not so much for his chivalry as for his primitive heroism, his readiness to risk himself with his men as Robert the Bruce had done. The Bruce had been praised

> . . . that he
> Is of sic will and sic bounte
> That he dar put him till assay* . . .[11]

It was this quality in James IV that Ayala misunderstood, and that aroused the admiration of an English chronicler

---

* risk himself.

who wrote "Oh what a noble and triumphant courage was this, for a King to fight in a battle as a mean soldier!"

The Scots followed their King with disastrous heroism. James IV died, not at the last surrounded by an impenetrable wood of spears, but early in the battle, charging downhill with his spearmen, who when their impetus had been halted found their long weapons useless against the shorter bills of the English, which could slice through the hafts of the Scottish spears and then be used to cut to pieces the defenceless spearmen. Among the many Scottish dead, disfigured by the terrible gashes of the English bills, the body of James IV was only identified with much difficulty.

According to contemporary records those who were slain with the King included one archbishop, two bishops, three abbots, one dean, fourteen Earls, about the same number of lords, three Highland Chiefs, and a great number of lairds, variously estimated. But modern research has tended to reduce earlier estimates of the number of the nameless dead, and to minimize the effect of the disaster upon the popular mind. Recent historians discredit the traditional picture of a nation distracted with grief, and point out that laments for "The Flowers of the Forest" are products of the romanticism of a later period. The loss which cannot be minimized in its effects, however, was the loss of the King. It was the loss of a strong King whose successes were personal, and whose achievements would inevitably be partially undone during the minority of his son.

James V, fated like his predecessors to succeed as a minor, was so far the youngest of his family to succeed. He was seventeen months old. The circumstances of his accession made it inevitable that he would face again many of the problems which had faced his predecessors, certainly the problems inherent in a minority. In addition he would have to face a new problem with the awakening of the Reformation, which would bring about new divisions in the Kingdom, to add to the difficulties which existing divisions perennially caused. He inherited, however, one great advantage: the prestige of the monarchy. Not one among the child Kings of Scots had been made away in the interests of an ambitious kinsman, like Edward V of England. The person of the King of Scots was sacred, as long as he had offended no man.

Chapter Two

THE KING'S MINORITY

What great misrule in to this region rang*
When our young prince could neither speak nor
gang† . . .
Some time our Queen rang‡ in authority
Some time the prudent Duke of Albany.
Sir David Lindsay "The Testament of the Papyngo."

KING JAMES V was the fourth child of his parents and the
only one to reach maturity. He was born on the evening
of Easter Saturday, 10th April 1512, in the Palace of Linlithgow. And at Linlithgow his mother Queen Margaret
Tudor received the news of the defeat of Flodden and the
death of her husband. Immediately she summoned the
Estates of the Realm, the Scottish Parliament, to meet at
Stirling, where the coronation of the new king was performed on 21st September in the Chapel Royal. The ceremony was performed with traditional splendour, but it
was overshadowed with such grief for James IV that it
was remembered as "the Mourning Coronation". At
first sight it seems arbitrary to signalize one among the
coronations of the Stewart Kings as a more mournful occasion than the rest; doubtless the popularity of James IV,
greater than that of any of his predecessors, and the extreme
youth of James V, which promised many years of disorder,
accounted for it. After the coronation the little King remained at Stirling Castle, and for him the next two years
passed uneventfully.

James IV, in a will made before the Flodden campaign,

* reigned in this country   † could neither talk nor walk.   ‡ reigned.

had appointed Queen Margaret tutrix, or guardian, of their son, in the event of his death, for so long as she should remain a widow. The parliament which met at Stirling in September ratified the appointment of the Queen to this position, which made her effectively the head of State, although she did not enjoy the title of regent. Margaret did not assume her position unopposed. A considerable party among the nobility, looking back to the history of previous minorities, was of the opinion that Scotland was not a country to be managed by a woman. According to Scottish theory, the king's nearest adult male kinsman should be regent; a theory which imposed an extremely heavy burden upon the loyalty of an ambitious man. In accordance with this theory the proper regent for James V was John, Duke of Albany, son of Alexander Duke of Albany, the brother of James III.

That the offering of the regency to Albany was an idea which could command any support is indicative not only of doubts of a woman's capacity to govern but also of dissatisfaction with the choice of Margaret as head of state.

Margaret had arrived in Scotland in 1503 to be received by James IV with great splendour and ceremony. In honour of their marriage the poet William Dunbar wrote "the Thistle and the Rose", celebrating the union of the two royal houses; and in an elegant lyric which was set to music and sung at the marriage festivities, he praised both Margaret's high birth and her beauty:

> Now fair, fairest of every fair,
> Princess most pleasant and preclare,
> The lustiest* one alive that been
>   Welcome to Scotland to be Queen . . .
>
> Sweet lusty luesome† Lady clear
> Most mighty Kinges daughter dear,
> Born of a princess most serene
>   Welcome to Scotland to be Queen . . .

* loveliest   † lovesome.

But behind the myth that all queens are beautiful the truth was that Margaret was far from being fairest of every fair. Dunbar offered the extravagant compliments that courtly convention demanded to a girl who would have been plain but for her bright colouring and the freshness of youth. No contemporary portrait of her has survived, but Daniel Mytens, a court painter to James VI and I and Charles I, painted for one of them a portrait of their ancestress based on a contemporary likeness. It shows Margaret richly and rather sombrely dressed in the fashion of the 1520's, incongruously posed against a conventional seventeenth century background, a plump, white-skinned woman with her red hair tucked into a jewelled French hood. She has a round face, rather bovine eyes and a soft, sensual mouth. Her almost subdued expression is perhaps the fault of the copyist, for nothing in her face suggests the wilful and imperious temper which directed her conduct after her husband's death.

In 1513 the lords of Scotland doubtless realised that Margaret possessed a strong will and an undisciplined intelligence, but a more powerful reason for their finding her unsuitable as head of state was that throughout the years that she had lived in Scotland she had never attempted to identify herself with her adoptive country. At heart she remained an Englishwoman, and was the affectionate sister of the king who had just inflicted upon Scotland so disastrous a defeat.

That king, "who regarded himself as heir to the Plantagenets, and who added to the tradition of the middle ages the realism of the renaissance, would have been less than his ancestors if he had failed to seek his profit in the occasion . . ."[1] The tradition of the middle ages had been for English Kings to claim suzerainty over the Kings of Scots, a claim which dated back to the capture of the Scottish King William the Lion in 1174. It had been renewed frequently since that date and when pressed by Edward I with all his military resources it had come perilously near to being made a reality. In 1513 Henry VIII had said to the herald of James IV who visited him in France before the Flodden campaign, "Thus say to thy master, that I am the very owner of Scotland, and he holdeth it of me by homage." Henry's renaissance realism came uppermost after James IV's death, when Henry realised that the supremacy he desired might be more effectively achieved by a less direct approach. Accordingly he claimed only to be recognized as "Protector of Scotland", as the uncle of the infant King. The Scottish Estates refused Henry that title, but the fear remained that with Margaret as head of state his influence would still extend itself over the country. Nonetheless, though the Duke of Albany might be the proper regent, and preferable to the Queen, his background was scarcely more confidence inspiring than hers.

Albany had been born and had always lived in France, the country to which his father, Alexander, had been banished by James III. Alexander, ambitious and disloyal, had been driven towards this fate by the persistence of his attempts to supplant his brother on the throne of Scotland. Defeated and banished, he had recouped his fortune beyond his deserts by marrying the immensely rich Agnès de la Tour d'Auvergne, daughter of the Comte de Boulogne, by whom he was the father of one son, John. In 1485 Alexander had met his end, killed accidentally at a tournament, and John, Duke of Albany, was brought up by his mother in France, unable to speak a word of Scots. It came to him naturally to think of himself as "Jehan Stuart" rather than John Stewart, to refer to the King of France as "mon maistre", and to regard France as his native country. In 1505 he married his maternal first cousin Anne de la Tour, Comtesse d'Auvergne. As a *grand seigneur* of France Albany led a life which seems to have satisfied every taste and ambition; he was highly regarded, and he was the friend of François, Comte d'Angoulême, who in due course became King François Ier of France.

Those members of the Scottish nobility who wished to limit the influence of Margaret Tudor were therefore prepared to set above her as regent a man of uncommendable antecedents who was a complete foreigner. They wrote to Albany with a preliminary invitation before the end of 1513.

Margaret's precarious position was at first strongly supported by popular sentiment. The energy with which she had summoned the Estates after Flodden and crowned the King inspired general admiration; and she became all the more an object of popular sympathy when it was learnt that she was pregnant by James IV. In April 1514 she gave birth to his posthumous son, Alexander, Duke of Ross, who survived less than two years. However, with the Chancellor James Beaton, Archbishop of Glasgow, the High Chamberlain Lord Home, and the Earl of Arran, the King's nearest kinsman after Albany, all eager for Albany's appointment as regent, Margaret could not rely upon popular sentiment alone to support her. She was driven to depend increasingly upon the Douglases, who were at emnity with her opponents, to help her retain her position.

The titular head of the powerful house of Douglas was Archibald, sixth Earl of Angus, who had recently succeeded his grandfather, his father having been killed at Flodden. Angus, though he was "childish young" and was described by his uncle the poet Gavin Douglas as "a young witless fool," was a member of Queen Margaret's council. Fortunately for his chances in the world he had various ambitious relatives to offer him advice, including his younger but more sage and mature brother, Sir George Douglas, his maternal grandfather Lord Drummond, and Gavin Douglas, who was a favourite counsellor of the Queen's. The substance of their advice could not be in doubt, for Margaret was surrounded by opponents and in need of a husband with a strong following of "dependers" to protect her interests. Her popularity with the commons received a severe blow, when on 6th August 1514, she married Angus, "for her plesour" as Bishop Lesley wrote later and everyone believed at the time.

Margaret, who was to repent of her marriage with remarkable rapidity, may have married Angus under duress, or at least under considerable pressure, for the marriage was performed secretly and the officiating priest was a Douglas. But if she married "for her plesour" her choice shows how little she had identified herself with the Stewart dynasty; for had she done so she would never have contemplated marrying a Douglas. Throughout the fifteenth century the Douglases had been the most dangerous rivals of the royal family, and by marrying Angus at the beginning of her son's minority Margaret Tudor assisted the Douglases to rival the power of the Stewarts afresh. Furthermore, Margaret's marriage played into the hands of the partisans of Albany, who were enabled to inform her that under the terms of James IV's will, by which she had been appointed guardian of the King only for so long as she should remain a widow, she had automatically forfeited her charge, and with it her position as head of state. While she privately resolved to retain the custody of both the King and his brother, Margaret was obliged to give her reluctant consent to the appointment of Albany as regent.[2]

By one of those sudden shifts of political alignment which characterize the complicated course of European politics in the first half of the sixteenth century, France had by this time become the ally of England. The alliance was sealed by the marriage of Henry VIII's younger sister Mary to Louis XII, the ageing King of France. Louis XII, to oblige his ally, prevented the departure of Albany for Scotland until the end of the year. But the death of Louis on the last day of 1514 freed Albany to depart. The policy of the new French King, François Ier, was shaped throughout his reign by his rivalry with the imperial house of

Henry VIII by an unknown artist

James V by an unknown artist

Habsburg on the battlefields of Europe. While, from time
to time, he required the alliance of England, he was not
disposed to drop the auld alliance with Scotland easily.
France had found it too useful in the past. Accordingly he
despatched Albany to Scotland, not, as the lords of Albany's
party had first expected, with men and munitions to continue the war with Henry VIII, but with advice to seek
peace. In the ratification of his predecessor's peace with
England, which François signed after his accession, Scotland
was included, though on disadvantageous and indeed
insulting terms; for while England was allowed to take
reprisals for Scottish border raids without infringing the
terms of the peace, the same concession was not allowed
to Scotland.

No natural inclinations had turned Albany's thoughts
towards Scotland. He accepted the regency when it was
offered him more as a duty to the auld alliance than with any
sense of gratification; and having assumed it he endeavoured
to reconcile the duty which he owed to James V with that
which he felt towards François Ier. The task was to prove almost impossible, and, not unpredictably, thankless. The
feuds of the Scottish nobility, the intrigues of Queen
Margaret and her new husband Angus, and the machina-
tions of the English ministers employed by Henry VIII to
increase Albany's difficulties, drove him at times to extremes
of passionate ill-temper. It was said that when provoked
beyond endurance he would snatch off his hat and fling it
into the fire. He solaced himself with hawking and hunting
when he had time, and in winter he managed to enjoy his
comforts – music, wine and warmth – at a price which bore
heavily on the exchequer. However, he made himself
respected as a ruler who "knew how to use men as they
are"; and considering that he was to all effects a total
foreigner, expensive to maintain, and committed to a
policy which did not enjoy universal support, he was
surprisingly popular with the nation which, for some years,

made his life burdensome. Albany arrived in Scotland on 18th May 1515, and having been welcomed with a great show of deference and rejoicing, he was escorted to Edinburgh, and ceremonially installed as regent on 10th July.

Upon his arrival Queen Margaret understandably received him as an enemy. His appointment as regent had marked the extinction of her authority, and, unacquainted with Scoltand as he was, he had grasped one of the basic facts of Scottish politics: that whoever held the King's person possessed the reality of power. Accordingly Albany demanded custody of the King, and of the Duke of Ross who might otherwise be used as a pawn against him. Furthermore he deprived Margaret of her advisers, with whom he dealt promptly and deftly: Lord Drummond he imprisoned in Blackness Castle, for striking the Lord Lyon King of Arms, a slender but sufficient pretext; Gavin Douglas he immured in the sea tower of St Andrews Castle, for illegally attempting to secure appointment to the archbishopric of St Andrews, made vacant by the death of the Archbishop at Flodden. But Margaret was not daunted. From the strong position of Stirling Castle, where she had kept the King since his coronation, she attempted to defy the regent, and refused to surrender her children.

Albany then sought to conciliate her, and he summoned the Estates through which he issued a modified demand: four lords, of whom Margaret should have the choice of three, should receive the King and his brother into their custody. Margaret, still resolved to keep her children, though uncertain how she could contrive to do so, made her nominations; but when the lords came to Stirling to claim their charges her response took them by surprise. The King made his first public appearance, standing hand in hand with his mother within the main gateway of the castle; but upon the approach of the lords the portcullis was dropped before them, and Margaret, from the other side of it, asked more time to consider the demand of the Estates before she parted with her children. Angus, who was beside her, at this point urged her to concede, and part with them. His failure to support her must have come as a shock to Margaret. Perhaps she subsequently saw it as the first of his many betrayals, which within a short time brought her to regard him as an enemy.

Upon the failure of his conciliatory move Albany prepared to besiege Margaret in Stirling Castle. He summoned the nobility to bring contingents to his assistance. Angus, who left his pregnant wife to face the prospect of a siege without him, decided to adopt a neutral position and declined to support the regent with his following. At this point Margaret could scarcely be blamed for looking to England for support, or at least for sympathy. She habitually corresponded with her brother and his ministers, setting out at length, and apparently without reserve, her thoughts, fears, intentions and complaints – thus filling the role of the English government's most highly placed secret agent in Scotland. As she awaited the approach of the besiegers she informed Lord Dacre, the English Warden of the Marches, that when they reached Stirling she intended to make the King stand in a prominent place on the castle walls wearing the crown, so that Albany's supporters should be forced to realize that they had taken up arms against their sovereign.[3] However, this vigorous illustration of defective logic was never seen. Albany, who appeared before Stirling on 4th August, in addition to bringing a force variously estimated at 7,000 or 8,000 men, brought the great gun Mons Meg, the most prestigious piece of ordnance of the age, calculated to strike terror to the defenders of any stronghold. Margaret made haste to surrender with a good grace. Again she came to the gates of the castle, hand in hand with the three year old James V, to whom she gave the keys, which he, walking forward alone, presented to Albany.

James and the Duke of Ross, parted from their mother, were left at Stirling in the charge of the Earl Marischal,

one of her previous nominees, and of the Lords Fleming
and Borthwick, with Lord Erskine as governor of the castle.
Queen Margaret, who did not see James until almost two
years later, and never saw her younger son again, was
escorted to the castle of Edinburgh. The regent's residence
was James IV's unfinished Palace of Holyroodhouse. Albany, who had acted in accordance with political necessity
in securing control of the King, was prudent in keeping his
distance from him, since his enemies found it easy, by
reviving the memory of the treasons of his father, to hint
that Albany himself might have designs upon the throne
of Scotland. After the regent had parted her from her
children these suspicions came naturally to the mind of
Margaret, and they were fostered by Lord Dacre, who,
before she was besieged at Stirling, had urged her to
attempt flight to England with her children. Dacre now
renewed his persuasions, and Margaret prepared to follow
his advice. She failed in an attempt to abduct her sons, but
nevertheless, feeling that her own position in Scotland had
become intolerable, and trusting that James and his brother
would be safe enough in the hands of the four lords until
another attempt could be made to spirit them away, she
resolved to make her own escape.

Margaret was now pregnant, and it was her pregnancy
which provided her with the means to effect an escape. On
20th August she announced her intention to "take her
chamber" at Linlithgow, ostensibly to remain in seclusion
with her ladies until the birth of her child. Thence she
slipped away to join Angus and his brother Sir George
Douglas, who had compromised themselves with the
Regent by refusing to follow him to Stirling. With an
escort of forty horsemen provided by Lord Home they
brought her safely to Blackadder Castle, one of Home's
strongholds. After waiting some time for Henry VIII's
permission to enter England they made their way to Lord
Dacre's castle of Harbottle in Northumberland, into

which Dacre received Margaret on 30th September, though he refused to admit Angus or any other Scot. On 7th October, in conditions of great discomfort and after a long and painful labour, Margaret gave birth to the only child of her marriage with Angus – Lady Margaret Douglas, famous to posterity as the mother of Lord Darnley and the ancestress of the Stewart dynasty of England.

As soon after her confinement as possible Margaret removed from Harbottle to Lord Dacre's principal castle at Morpeth, where comforts could be more easily provided for her. To Morpeth came Sir Christopher Garneys, sent by Henry VIII with presents for his sister. Sir Christopher somewhat unkindly criticized Margaret's extravagant enthusiasm for these presents, gowns "of cloth of gold and tinsen"* and her excitement at the prospect of displaying herself in all this splendour as soon as her health would permit her to travel to the English court.

Albany, meanwhile, discovered that all his difficulties had not been ended by the flight of Margaret and the securing of the custody of the King and his brother. In the autumn of 1515 Albany faced a rebellion led by Lord Home who had been the most eager among the lords for his appointment as regent, and was the earliest to become disillusioned with him. Home was "a man unpolisht, stubbornly stout, hazardous, mighty in riches and power and consequently proud." He had enjoyed considerable influence in the previous reign, and possibly he expected to increase his power under the regency of a man inexperienced in Scottish politics. Albany probably forfeited his support when he proved less amenable to his influence than Home had hoped. After the escape of Queen Margaret, which Home was known to have abetted, Albany placed him in ward in the custody of the Earl of Arran. By birth Arran was a great

---

* tinsen or tinsel was 'a rich sparkling fabric of silk interwoven with gold or silver thread. It might be coloured crimson, green or black.' *Handbook of English Costume in the Sixteenth Century* by C. W. and F. Cunnington.

personage, whose position as a grandson of James II and nephew of James III commanded respect; what Albany had not realized was that Arran's mental processes did not command respect, except perhaps for their remarkable complexity. Intelligent, but disastrously suggestible, he was ever at the mercy of a stronger personality or of a persuasive tongue. Not only did Home induce Arran to abet his escape, he induced him to escape with him. The next that Albany heard of both gaoler and prisoner was that they had fled to the west, where, joined by Angus, they gathered a group of associates which included the Earls of Lennox and Glencairn, and signed a "band" to deliver the King and his brother from the Regent's custody. Albany retaliated with decision. Before the rebels had time to consolidate their position he marched to the west, laid seige to Arran's stronghold of Hamilton, and quickly had the whole rebellion under control. He then showed his opponents a clemency designed to win their support. Arran he pardoned, and Lord Home and his brother William were pardoned on condition of their future good behaviour. Angus fled and rejoined Margaret in Northumberland; but he shortly regretted his decision, for the clemency of Albany was comprehensive. Lord Drummond and Gavin Douglas were out of prison now, and Douglas, in compensation for his failure to obtain the archbishopric of St Andrews, had been appointed to the see of Dunkeld. Angus, preferring on second thoughts the prospect of a share in Albany's goodwill to a share in Margaret's exile, abandoned her and returned to Scotland, where he was well received by the regent. In the spring of 1516, when Margaret journeyed to the English court, she complained bitterly to her brother of Angus's defection. "Done like a Scot!" was Henry VIII's characteristic rejoinder.

It was not long before the uneasy tranquillity which followed Albany's conciliatory measures was broken again by the activities of Lord Home. Treasonable intercourse with England, designed to weave around Albany "an inextricable web of intrigue and faction"[4] led to the arrest of both Home and his brother, who were tried for high treason in the autumn of 1516. It is probable that besides discovering Home's renewed intrigues Albany had listened to tales of his dubious conduct at the conclusion of the previous reign, told him by Home's arch-enemy John Hepburn, Prior of St Andrews, a man "of subtle mind, malicious, crafty . . . and undued with some courtly eloquence", who was much in Albany's confidence. Albany had evidently been impressed as much by old gossip as by new revelations, for at Home's trial, James, Earl of Moray, a bastard son of the late King, appeared to accuse Home of having murdered James IV after Flodden. But the charge was dropped for lack of evidence, and both the Homes were condemned to death for their treasons against the regent. Lord Home was executed on 8th October and his brother on the following day.

The triumph of Albany over all opposition in Scotland appeared to be complete. The strength of his position had been illustrated earlier in the year when Henry VIII had written to the Scottish Estates in support of a demand addressed by Margaret to Albany that she should be restored to her position as head of state; for in reply to Henry's demand that Albany should be dismissed from his regency and sent back to France, the Estates had returned a firm refusal, in which they declared their satisfaction with the way in which Albany had acquitted himself since reluctantly leaving France to take up the regency. In November 1516 Albany further strengthened what already seemed to be an unassailable position by inducing the Estates to grant him official recognition as "Second Person" or heir presumptive to the Scottish throne; after which he felt sufficiently secure to contemplate paying a visit to France, to attend both to his family affairs and to the foreign affairs of Scotland.

It was April 1517 before the Estates could be persuaded to agree to Albany's departure, and June had come before he was able to leave Scotland. Shortly after his arrival in France Albany negotiated a favourable treaty for Scotland with François Ier. In 1516 François had signed with King Charles of Spain (later the Emperor Charles V) a treaty in which he promised Charles his eldest daughter Louise, or should she die before the marriage could take place, his second daughter Charlotte. In August 1517 Albany exacted from François an agreement that Charlotte should marry James V, or, if Charles should claim her, that James should marry the next daughter born to the Queen of France. This was not a hypothetical treaty, for by the time it was ratified in 1521 it had been given substance by the birth of the necessary third princess. In addition to the matrimonial clauses there was also provision for an offensive and defensive alliance between Scotland and France. The long gap between the negotiation and the ratification of the Treaty of Rouen was caused by the four years absence of Albany from Scotland; for he was detained in France, as he had been before he took up his regency, by an Anglo-French *rapprochement*. It was not until after the collapse of the brittle alliance between François Ier and Henry VIII that Albany was able to return to Scotland.

In the meantime Scotland had been experiencing again the force of a truism which the past had made bitterly familiar: "Woe to the land where the King is a child."

The first crime of violence following the regent's departure, which was outrageous even in a country where murderous feuds were commonplace, was the murder of Antoine d'Arces, Sieur de la Bastie, the Frenchman whom Albany had made Warden of the Marches and president of the council of regency appointed to govern Scotland in his absence.

Around the unfortunate La Bastie was the aura of a mediaeval romance. He had first come to Scotland as a contestant in the magnificent tournaments held by James IV, having toured Europe with a challenge to all comers to combat *à l'outrance* (i.e. mortal combat), "for my pleasure, and following the virtues and prowess of the ancient valourous knights of past times."[5] He was so exceptionally handsome that many Scots, unfamiliar with the construction of French surnames, supposed him to be called "Sir de la Beautie". He wore his hair very long, in the fashion of the preceding century, to which, in spirit, he belonged. It was an unhappy destiny which made so quixotic a person Albany's Warden of the Marches, and embroiled him in blood feuds instead of tournaments. Decoyed from the castle of Dunbar by a false report of a border incident, he was waylaid and set upon by the Homes. His horse carried him into a swamp, and there he was surrounded and his head was hacked off as a reprisal for Albany's execution of Lord Home. As the completion of this act of savagery, Home of Wedderburn tied the head to his saddle by its long hair, and rode with it to the town of Duns, where he exhibited it in triumph on a spear.

The crime excited considerable horror in Scotland, grieved and angered Albany, and deeply offended François Ier; but, for all the feeling it aroused, it went unpunished, largely because Arran, the premier nobleman in Albany's absence, was unwilling to make an example of the Homes, with whom he was connected. The Council of Regency rapidly divided into factions, and in the absence either of justice or of leadership the condition of the country declined into chaos.

The two principal agents of disorder were the Earls of Arran and Angus. Arran, territorially powerful and influential by reason of his descent, though personally incompetent, had vigorous supporters, of whom the most formidable was his bastard son Sir James Hamilton of Finnart. Angus, naturally ambitious as head of the house of Douglas, if he had ever been the "young witless fool" his uncle

Gavin Douglas thought him, had not long remained so. His ability had grown with his ambition, and it outmatched the ability of Arran. In estates and followings they were less unequal. Arran's close kinship to the King made the pretensions of Angus intolerable to him and disposed him to support Albany; Angus's marriage to Queen Margaret conversely disposed him to be a partisan of England. Thus the old feud of Douglas and Hamilton became enlarged in scope into a feud of "English" and "French" factions. The ensuing disorder resulted in several outbreaks of violence, culminating in a street battle in Edinburgh in April 1520, popularly remembered as "Cleanse the Causeway", in which a small party of Douglases drove a much larger force of Hamiltons out of the city. The name of the battle came perhaps from the rallying cry adopted that day by the Douglases. The defeated Arran and Hamilton of Finnart only escaped by fording the Nor' Loch both on one horse, which they had cut loose from a cart. The condition of the country was piteously described as past all care but the help of God, by the author of "An Orison when the Governor past in France":

> We are so beastly, dull and ignorant
> Our rudeness may not lightly be correctit . . .
> And in folly we are so far infectit
> That, but thy help, this kynrick is folorn . . .[6]

The strife of factions was mirrored in little by the strife of Angus and Margaret, who had returned to Scotland when Albany departed. Both of them desired power and each disliked the masterful temper of the other. Rivalry for power would have been cause enough to ensure future trouble between them; but it was not long before Margaret discovered specific reasons for resentment against her husband. The first of his offences to be revealed was that he had appropriated the rents from her dower lands in Ettrick Forest which, she wrote "ought to bring me in

4,000 merks yearly, and I shall never get a penny."[7] But even more unforgivable was the next revelation. Margaret learnt that in her absence Angus had taken as his mistress the woman he had once intended to marry, Janet Stewart, daughter of the laird of Traquair.

By 1519 Margaret was exploring the possibility of divorcing Angus. Her first idea was to secure the support of her brother for the project; but when she wrote to Henry VIII, far from supporting her, he berated her for contemplating divorce, which he condemned as an immoral and non-Christian proceeding. He sent a cleric, Henry Chadworth, to effect a reconciliation between Margaret and her husband; he looked to Margaret and Angus to provide solidarity for the English party in Scotland. Margaret outwardly acquiesced to Chadworth's arguments, but in obstinacy she was the equal of Henry VIII. If he used her in such an unbrotherly fashion, she resolved, both for spite and for an effective remedy, to have recourse to the enemy. Accordingly she initiated a friendly correspondence with the Duke of Albany. He could help her if he would, he was *persona grata* at the court of Rome, and his influence there had recently been increased by the marriage of his wife's sister Madeleine de la Tour to the Pope's nephew, Lorenzo de Medici, Duke of Urbino.

In 1521 the international situation permitted Albany to return to Scotland. The Anglo-French alliance crumbled rapidly after the meeting of Henry VIII and François Ier at the Field of Cloth of Gold – a meeting which served rather to indicate their essential rivalry than, as had been intended, to illustrate their friendship. During 1521 Henry VIII reached an agreement with the Emperor Charles V that they should make a concerted attack on France; and therefore, at the end of the year, François sent Albany to Scotland to be prepared to administer that thrust in the back of England which was the traditional action the French Kings required of their Scottish allies.

Albany arrived on 29th November 1521, to find that his former enemy Margaret, now that she entertained such hopes of him, had become his warmest supporter. Inevitably this sudden warmth between two enemies provided scope for scandal, and Henry VIII was soon informed that Albany and Margaret were closeted together half the day and half the night, and that it was suspected they were "over tender". Albany's return to Scotland had sufficiently angered Henry, but the scandal incensed him even further. In January 1522 the current Anglo-Scottish truce for one year was due to expire, and Henry's hasty action upon the pretext thus provided played neatly into Albany's hands. Henry sent Clarencieux Herald to Scotland with letters thunderously accusing Albany of the "damnable abusing of our sister", and with instruction to inform the Scottish Estates that the truce would not be renewed unless Albany were expelled from Scotland.

Albany's reply to the accusation that he had seduced the Queen was crushing in the extreme. "The King of England," he told Clarencieux in the presence of the Estates, "need not misdoubt he would attempt anything should derogate from the honour of his sister, that compliments of mere courtesy in France might be surmised sometimes by English ladies to be solicitations and suits of love." So much for that. As far as his expulsion from Scotland was concerned, if Albany had lacked a good reason to induce the Scots to go to war with England on François Ier's behalf, this unreasonable demand of Henry VIII provided exactly what he needed. The Scots were not willing to part with Albany. His achievement in enforcing law and order during his first period of residence in Scotland seemed all the greater by contrast with the chaos which had ensued upon his absence. Since his return his supporters had achieved a strong ascendancy over the Douglas-dominated pro-English group. (1522 saw Angus in France, temporarily banished, and Gavin Douglas at the English court, ensuring that Henry VIII's mind became increasingly poisoned against Albany's regime.) Albany therefore commanded strong enough support to lead a military expedition against England in July 1522.

Circumstances combined to make Albany's expedition a fiasco. Henry VIII invaded France, so that it became obvious that Scotland was going to war more on François's behalf than upon her own. And Margaret Tudor, who never felt so much an Englishwoman as when Scotland went to war with England, betrayed Albany's plans to Lord Dacre. When the Army reached Carlisle the militancy aroused by Henry VIII's ultimatum earlier in the year had completely evaporated, and Flodden loomed large in the minds of all who had followed Albany. None was willing that Scotland should make another such sacrifice for the sake of the auld alliance. The Scottish commanders declined to lead the army across the Border. Albany was thankful for the opportunity offered by Lord Dacre to conclude a temporary truce. Dacre had no authority to do so, but his action was from the English viewpoint a "felix culpa", as Wolsey put it.[8]

Albany returned to France in October 1522, to make clear to François Ier that if he looked for military action from the Scots he must send them military support. It seemed that Albany's second visit to Scotland had been an abortive one; but something of future importance had been done. Albany had caused the Estates to ratify the Treaty of Rouen; and when Albany returned to France François Ier also signed it. The treaty now had reality, for in 1520 the Princess Madeleine, the future bride of James V, had been born.

In November 1522 Henry VIII offered a five year truce and the hand of his daughter Mary for James V, on condition that Scotland repudiated Albany. But the Estates, having just committed Scotland to the French alliance and James to a French marriage, refused the offer. Henry retaliated with a renewal of hostilities against Scotland. In June 1523 Kelso was burnt, and on 24th September an

English force under the Earl of Surrey (the son of the victor of Flodden) burnt Jedburgh.

On the same day Albany once more landed in Scotland, bringing with him the military contingents supplied by François Ier. The cost of maintaining this force of 4,000 infantry, an unspecified number of arquebusiers and five or six hundred horses was probably what decided Albany to launch his campaign at once, in spite of the lateness of the year. It was unfortunate for him that winter set in early. By the time the army was marching south in late October the roads were almost impassable, especially for the artillery which François Ier had provided. Nonetheless, Albany was not deterred. He ordered the religious houses on his route to provide teams of oxen to haul the artillery through the mud.[9] When the Border was reached Albany found his commanders as unwilling to invade England as they had been the previous year. He managed to urge them across the river Tweed, and ordered an attack on Wark Castle. Although it was said of Albany that he had "small lucke . . . in feates of warre", he was not lacking in military sense. However high the morale of his army had been he would have been unwilling to invade England leaving a strong castle still in enemy hands behind his line of advance. But the morale of the Scots was low, and Albany doubtless hoped that if the castle were successfully stormed that small victory would encourage his army to advance into England. However, Wark held out, while the unenthusiastic Scots allowed the French contingent to do most of the fighting. Then, as the weather worsened the waters of the Tweed began to rise, and the English army under Surrey was rumoured to be approaching. Albany was forced to withdraw. His army marched back towards Edinburgh through a heavy snowstorm.[10] The bitter weather disposed both sides to a truce. But the English poet laureate, John Skelton, who had been Henry VIII's tutor, jubilantly ridiculed the discomfiture of the Scots:

Rejoyse, Englande
And understande
These tidinges newe
Whiche be as trewe
As the gospell:
This duke so fell
Of Albany
So cowardly,
With all his hoost
Of the Scottyshe Coost,
For all their boost
Fledde like a beest . . .
Ye shall trowe me
False Scottes are ye . . .
Like cowardes starke
At the castell of Warke,
By the water of Twede
Ye had evill spede;
Lyke cankered curres
Ye lost your spurres,
For in that fraye
Ye ranne away . . .
. . . ye and your hoost
Full of bragge and boost
And full of waste wynde
Howe ye wyll beres* bynd,
And the devill down dynge†
Yet ye dare do nothynge,
But lepe away lyke frogges,
And hyde you under logges,
Lyke pigges and lyke hogges
And lyke mangy dogges . . .

And so on, at interminable length, and in verse more disastrous than the discomfiture it mocked.

The French troops were not permitted to remain in Scotland over the winter; the cost of maintaining them was too great. Albany himself left Scotland in the spring of

* bears.   † strike down the devil.

47

1524, promising to return by 1st September on pain of forfeiting his regency. But he did not return then or thereafter. It is probable that he would have honoured his promise, but his services were required by François Ier in his Italian campaigns against the Emperor. François was defeated and captured at Pavia in 1525, and by the time Albany was again able to turn his thoughts towards Scotland his regency had been terminated and his opponents were in control.

The departure of Albany, his influence weakened by two ignominious military expeditions, left Scotland open to the designs of Henry VIII. The Scots did not appreciate that Albany's regency had saved the country from English domination. They realized that Scotland had been treated ungenerously by François Ier, but not that the French alliance had served a defensive purpose in spite of him. However, after Albany had gone Henry VIII did not have all his own way; the selfishness with which his supporters pursued their own ambitions ensured that they did not play his game to any greater extent than suited themselves.

The first to take advantage of Albany's departure was Margaret Tudor. She resolved to recover the position of power which she had enjoyed immediately after the death of James IV, and in projecting her *coup d'état* she found an ally in Arran, who in recent years had been a steady supporter of Albany. However, the death of the Duchess of Albany without surviving children had recently increased the importance of Arran *vis-à-vis* the Scottish succession, and acted as a spur to his ambition. It was fitting, he decided, that he should be as close to the King in power as he was in blood. Between them Margaret and Arran concerted a plan of action. They decided that the minority of James V and the regency of Albany should be declared formally at an end. The young King should be brought to Edinburgh and invested with the symbols of his sovereignty. Thereafter he should be the nominal ruler of Scotland, the reality of power being in the hands of his mother and her ally.

In accordance with this plan the twelve-year-old James was brought from Stirling Castle and, on 26th July 1524, invested by Arran with the crown, sceptre and sword of state. On 1st August James presided at a meeting of the privy council, at which the officers of state resigned their offices to him, and were for the most part immediately re-appointed. The coup was not achieved without opposition. Archbishop Beaton, the Chancellor (who since 1522 had been Archbishop of St Andrews and primate of Scotland) objected against the termination of Albany's regency before 1st September. Beaton's objection was supported by five bishops as well as by the Earls of Argyll, Lennox and Moray. Margaret and Arran, however, dealt shortly with the opposition. Archbishop Beaton and the Bishop of Aberdeen were imprisoned, and the rest were overawed by the show of force.

Margaret prepared to enjoy the sensation of power regained. But she was not alone in realizing that whoever possessed the King's person possessed power in Scotland. Her husband was equally aware of it, and equally deter-mined to exploit the situation to his own advantage.

Chapter Three

THE ASCENDANCY OF ANGUS

Then durst no man come neirhand the King
But the surname of the doughty Douglas
Which so royally in this region did ring* . . .

"Ane Deploratioun of King James the Fyft . . ." Lindsay *of Pitscottie. Derived, with variations, from Sir
David Lindsay's "The Testament of the Papyngo".*

"IT is delightful to understand every particular circumstance
in the progress of the actions of princes" wrote William
Drummond of Hawthornden in his account of the reign of
James V; but in the very instance of James V it is impossible
to do so for the first twelve years of the King's life. Only
when his formal education, and together with it his childhood,
had been brought peremptorily to an end by his mother's
coup d'état does it become possible to follow the progress
of his actions in any detail. Until that time the entries made
in official records which detail the provisions made for his
welfare, and the works of a poet who, fortunately for posterity, occupied a post close to the King, provide almost
all that we know of James V. However, this very scantiness
of information shows that James was fortunate in one
thing: during the troubled and violent years of his minority,
his own life was mercifully uneventful.

At Linlithgow Palace, and after his coronation, at Stirling, he grew from a baby into a small child without disturbances, until his mother brought him to confront the four
lords who demanded custody of him and the little Duke of

* reign.

50

Ross. When James was a baby he had as his nurse a woman named Christian Wille, who was replaced when he was a little older by a Mistress of the Household, Elizabeth Douglas, whose appointment was doubtless made about the time of Queen Margaret's marriage to Angus. At the same time the "rokkaris" of James's cradle were replaced by three "gentlewomen" to attend upon him.

At Stirling, after he had been parted from his mother, he was well guarded and conscientiously taken care of. When Albany left for France in 1517 he had the King removed from Stirling Castle to Edinburgh, as a place of even greater strength and safety. Albany's enemies did their best to spread the belief that James and his brother were neglected by the regent, in the hope that they would die, and Albany be thus enabled to make himself King. The Duke of Ross did indeed die, but certainly not from neglect, for the Treasurer's Accounts contain many entries detailing clothes and other things provided for him during his short life. Nonetheless Gavin Douglas in 1522 wrote Henry VIII a very circumstantial account of the treatment to which, according to him, James had been subjected at Albany's hands, in the hope that the young King would go the same way as his brother.

Douglas began by comparing Albany to Richard III, who had allegedly murdered his two nephews to clear his path to the throne. Incidentally, John Skelton, in his derisive poem upon Albany's unsuccessful seige of Wark castle, had inserted the accusation that Albany intended to murder and supplant the King:

> . . . ye pretende
> For to defende
> The younge Scottyshe Kyng.
> But ye meane a thynge,
> And ye could bryng
> The matter about,
> To putte his eyes out

And put hym downe,
And set hys crowne
On your owne heed
When he were deed.

Douglas improved upon these unpleasant lines by declaring, as a fact, that Albany had poisoned the Duke of Ross. But as far as the King was concerned, since no harm had come to him, Douglas was more guarded. He merely hinted at the Regent's intention by detailing his supposed ill-usage of the King – for example his removing him from Stirling to "the windy and right unpleasant castle and rock of Edinburgh." Furthermore, he described how "the King's rich gowns of most fine cloth of gold, furred with finest sables" and the hangings and furnishings of his bedchamber, of "purple and velvet cramosyn" had been taken by Albany and made into clothes for his pages. Then, somewhat inconsistently, Douglas went on to say that when Albany and Margaret sent the King cloth of gold and silver for gowns, the officers of the household, a bunch of rogues appointed by Albany, had refused to provide material for the linings.[1] The Treasurer's Accounts prove that all this was merely malicious propaganda, and that Albany provided properly for the King's needs. But for all Gavin Douglas's talk of cloth of gold, apart from a black velvet doublet with cloth of gold sleeves, most of James's clothes were warm and sensible garments made of various types of woollen material, in practical colours, usually grey, russet or black. Sometimes the clothes are described in considerable detail in the Treasurer's Accounts, but some of the descriptions are rather misleading. For instance it appears that many pairs of "skarlot" hose were made for James V. But "skarlot" was a type of woollen material, and in this context the word refers to the material and is not used as the name of a colour, which explains the existence of such odd-sounding stuff as "black skarlot". Russet, which was much used for the little King's clothes, was also the name of a woollen material that was sometimes grey in colour, sometimes the reddish-brown colour associated with the name.[2]

Besides providing for the King's needs a great deal more conscientiously than his enemies would admit, Albany seems wisely to have let the King's household arrangements continue as they had done under Margaret's regime. The parting with his mother must have been the most memorable event of James's early life, and, followed by the death of his small brother so soon afterwards, it must have given him a bleak sense of loss and loneliness. The Duke of Ross was said to have been Margaret's favourite child, and on hearing of his death she lamented him as "a marvellous sweet bairn and pleasant". But she showered affection upon both her sons, the only survivors of the five children that she had borne to James IV. Some years later she was criticized for spoiling the King "out of too much motherly kindness". However, when he was deprived of her attentions in 1515 it was fortunate that the routine workings of the household, which provided the reassuring background of his life, were little disrupted; fortunate also that he was surrounded by the familiar faces of his usual attendants, with some of whom he would probably have been more intimate than with his mother, since they, not she, would have been responsible for all the practical duties concerned with his upbringing.

All the other attendants that the King had, however, were made almost superfluous by the doting attention of his Master Usher, the poet Sir David Lindsay of the Mount. Lindsay has left a lively account of the King's early childhood, and of his own unwearying attendance upon and entertainment of him:

> When thou was young I bore thee in mine arme
> Full tenderly, till thou begouth to gang,*
> And in thy bed oft happit† thee full warme,
> With lute in hand, syne, sweetly to thee sang;

began to walk.   † wrapped.

> Some time in dancing, feiralie I flang;*
> And some time playing farces on the flure,
> And some time on mine office taking cure.[3]

It was indeed fortunate for the King that the loss of his father and the temporary removal of his mother did not mean that he was left without affection. The real devotion, the kindliness and good nature which David Lindsay showed James V were rewarded by the lifelong continuance of the King's favour and friendship. That Lindsay's charming entertainment had meant a very great deal to him, and that he was fond of the poet himself, is obvious. Lindsay describes how he used to amuse the little King, in a well-known passage of another poem:

> I take the Quenis grace, thy mother,
> My Lord Chancellor† and many other
> Thy nowreis‡ and thy auld maistres,§
> I take them all to bear witness . . .
> How, as a chapman bears his pack
> I bore they grace upon my back.
> And sometimes strydlingis** on my neck
> Dancing with many a bend and beck.
> The first sillabis that thou didst mute
> Was 'Pa Da Lyn' – upon the lute
> Then played I twenty springs perqueir¶
> When was great pity for to hear.
> From play thou let me never rest
> But 'Gynkertoun' thou loved, ay, best . . .
> I wat thou loved me better, than,
> Nor now some wife does her good man.[4]

It is a statement often repeated that Sir David Lindsay was tutor to James V. However, Lindsay's appointments were those of 'Master Usher', 'Keeper of the King's Person' and 'Master of the Household', offices which kept him

* wonderously I leapt.   † i.e. Archbishop Beaton.
‡ thy nurse, i.e. Christian Wille.
§ Mistress of the Household i.e. Elizabeth Douglas.
** astride.   ¶ i.e. par coeur – by heart.

always close to the King. There can be little doubt that James learnt a great deal from Lindsay's lively and cultivated mind, but Lindsay's connection with his education was informal. In one poem Lindsay admits that one of his functions was to provide light relief:

> And, ay, when thou came from the school
> Then I behuffit* to play the fool.

In another he describes the King's insatiable desire to be told stories, and reminds him of the tales which he had enjoyed:

> But, now, thou art by influence natural
> High of ingynet†, and right inquisitive
> Of antique stories and deeds martial.
> More pleasantly the time for to o'erdrive
> I have, at length, the stories done descrive
> Of Hector, Arthur and gentle Julius,
> Of Alexander, and worthy Pompeius,
>
> Of Jason and Medea, all at length,
> Of Hercules the actis honourable
> And of Samson the supernatural strength
> And of leill lovers stories amiable . . .[5]

While all this was as informative as it was entertaining, the schoolroom proper was presided over by Gavin Dunbar "ane young clerk", the nephew of Bishop Gavin Dunbar of Aberdeen. He probably had as an assistant the King's Chaplain, Sir James Inglis. Dunbar was specifically engaged to teach the King Latin and French; but though he was reputed to be very learned he did not pass on a great deal of his learning to James. He was principally concerned to give the King a good grounding in Latin, and probably James had become proficient enough in it by the time his formal education came to its premature end. He learnt to read and write French adequately, but his spoken French was never very fluent. If James V's education seems poor by

* It behoved me.
† Of high intelligence.

comparison with that of other renaissance princes and princesses – Henry VIII, Edward VI, Lady Jane Grey and Elizabeth Tudor, for example – it may be said in extenuation that his education ended at a very early age. On the other hand, some of the others mentioned had attained a much higher standard by the time they reached the age of twelve. Possibly James V would have been given a more thorough education if his father had lived longer, for James IV had been most highly educated. According to Ayala he spoke Latin "very well", French, German, Flemish, Italian and Spanish, besides Gaelic; he was interested in scientific experiments, in dentistry and surgery, and he was an accomplished musician. In this James V did not fall behind his father's attainments – or his mother's – for Margaret Tudor was also a good musician, as were most of the Tudors. James V's favoured instrument was the lute; that he practised assiduously is shown by many entries in the Treasurer's Accounts for the purchase of lutestrings. He could sight read well, and "sing that which he had never seen before – but his voice was rawky and harsh".[6]

James V also took after his father in his desire for and cultivation of athletic prowess. Indeed, he was essentially less interested in his books than in his horses and weapons. In horsemanship and martial sports, occupations considered as important as learning for a prince, it became his pleasure and determination to excel. And he did excel. When two English emissaries came to Edinburgh in the autumn following Queen Margaret's *coup d'état* of July 1524, James was obliged to show off his accomplishments to them. They saw him dancing and singing and "showing familiarity among his lords"; then, at an entertainment provided for them at Leith by Margaret, they saw him give a display of horsemanship. In all that he did, they reported to Henry VIII, "his princely acts and doings be so excellent for his age not yet of XIII years till Easter next that in our opinions it is not possible they should be amended" (bettered).[7] But if James impressed the emissaries with his display of accomplishments, personally he impressed them even more. He was a very good looking red-haired boy, and on the evidence of his coinage he still wore his hair long, a fashion which finally disappeared at the end of the 1520's. He was ill-tempered and violent, but he could be charming when he chose to be. To the emissaries he was very gracious. He showed the other side of his nature when he knifed the porter of Stirling Castle who refused to open the gates at his demand. The emissaries considered that he very much resembled Henry VIII, who at his age had been considered a paragon of princely beauty.

Henry VIII was interested in every detail of information concerning his nephew of Scotland. The two emissaries, whom he sent to be residents at the Scottish Court, were employed specifically to increase English influence there. Dr Magnus, "a great orator" was the principal, and the conveyor of Henry's wishes to Margaret and her allies; Roger Radcliffe, a gentleman of Henry's Privy Chamber, was expected to form a friendly relationship with the young King, and to influence him in favour of an English alliance. For a time it seemed that this would not be difficult. During Albany's regime James had been treated as a child, perpetually obliged to do as his guardians and tutors told him – the incident with the porter at Stirling suggests that he had latterly found the restraints of childhood unendurably frustrating. Since his mother's *coup d'état* he had begun to feel like a king – fêted, admired, the recipient of compliments and presents from his uncle's emissaries. It was not difficult to present the contrast to him as the contrast between Albany's attitude and Henry's, French and English. The effect upon his mind was shown when he wrote Henry a letter containing a derogatory reference to Albany "under whose governance our realm and lieges has been right evil 'demanyt' "*

* i.e. mismanaged.

This would have been eminently satisfactory to Henry. It will be remembered that at the outset of James V's minority he had endeavoured to claim the style of "Protector of Scotland", which the Estates had refused him; that he had intended to extend his influence over Scotland through Margaret is not in doubt. According to her most recent biographer Margaret saw herself as her brother's "vicereine" in Scotland,[8] a position which the Scottish nobility's preference for Albany had prevented her from obtaining, and one which she intended to attain as a result of her *coup d'état*. Henry had every intention of assisting her, which he did to the extent of sending a guard of two hundred English archers, paid by himself, to protect his nephew's person. But his protection had a sinister aspect, for his true attitude to Scotland had been shown long ago when he had declared to James IV's herald "I am the very owner of Scotland, and he (James IV) holdeth it of me by homage . . ." While this attitude could not be other than outrageous to James V, when he should become aware of it, to Queen Margaret, as a Tudor and an Englishwoman it was entirely acceptable. Henry VIII, however, was aware that Margaret herself had not been an acceptable head of state to the majority of the Scottish nobility, and that, having regained her position, it would be no easier for her to retain it than it had previously been. He was therefore anxious to see her reconciled with Angus, which would put her and Angus together at the head of a strong party.

* * *

The end of Albany's regency enabled Angus to leave his French exile. He was no longer the violent young factionary that Albany had banished. While he remained ready to resort to violence when it seemed advantageous, his character had gained an extra dimension of patience and astuteness. He returned to Scotland by way of the English court, where he was very favourably received by Henry VIII.

On his return to Scotland he expressed with great humility his desire for a reconciliation with Margaret. But Margaret was recalcitrant. When he entered Edinburgh she and Arran defended the castle, while Angus and the Earl of Lennox took possession of the town. Margaret had the King with her, and Angus could not avoid looking like a rebel. But Margaret's refusal of a reconciliation had put her in the wrong in her brother's eyes. Henry set a higher value on Angus's ability to deal with the lords of Scotland than upon hers, and Angus would, he was assured, serve England better than Margaret's principal ally Arran – in fact "better than five Earls of Arran."[9] Margaret was obliged, for the second time within a few years, to submit to a formal reconciliation with Angus; but she refused him his conjugal rights, for she was more determined than ever to divorce him, and was indeed already preparing to do so.

Margaret's divorce petition was a curious one, based on the myths which grew up concerning James IV after his death at Flodden. The love which he had inspired, and the memory of his reign as something like a Golden Age by comparison with the disordered minority of James V, made many of the people unwilling to accept the fact of his death. In the manner of King Arthur, and indeed of many other legendary heroes, James IV was popularly believed not to have been slain, but to have disappeared, to return at his kingdom's need. The most prosaic version of this myth was that he had gone disguised on a pilgrimage to the Holy Land. Margaret seized upon the myth of his survival, and pleaded that, at the time of her marriage to Angus, James IV was known by others, though not by herself, to have been alive.

Margaret entrusted the management of the divorce proceedings to Albany, who generously undertook the business and obtained her what she wanted in 1525. She had good reason to be grateful for his generosity: not only did he obtain the divorce from the Pope, which possibly no one else could have done, but he also paid for it. Doubtless he did not arrange the divorce from motives of pure altruism. He did not lose his interest in Scottish affairs, which he continued to look after in France and at Rome. He must have hoped that the divorce of Margaret and Angus would loosen the tie between Angus and Henry VIII, and so undermine English influence in Scotland. It was not much to the purpose, for Henry VIII continued to support Angus, while he "never carried such respect to his sister as he had done before." Margaret, however, was thankful to be free of the man she had long ago come to detest. Angus no longer needed her to further his ambition. He had the support of Henry who was confident both of his ability and his willingness to rule Scotland as England's ally and satellite. All that he needed was to possess the King.

Following his formal reconciliation with Margaret in March 1525, he became a member of her council, over which he quickly gained control. In July it was arranged that the custody of the King should be given to a rota of four lords, each of whom would be responsible for him for a quarter of the year. They were to be Angus, Arran, Lennox and Argyll. The coup which ended Margaret's short-lived recovery of power was of extreme simplicity. Angus took up responsibility first, but when the time came for him to hand over the King to the next lord of the rota in November 1525, he refused to do so. The King, so recently released from the trammels of childhood, found himself far more frustratingly entrammelled in a condition very like imprisonment.

Margaret and Arran accused Angus of treason for "invassalling his Prince to his attendance." Angus did not even deign to reply; but he caused his brother Sir George Douglas to force the King to write an answer. James was compelled to write to his mother to the effect that "with none more cheerfully, willingly and contentedly could he live and spend his time than with the Earl of Angus."

This was far from the truth; having experienced first constraint and then compulsion, he was desperate to get back to the indulgent care of his mother and Arran. He managed to write to them secretly, begging them to free him from Angus, and "if it could not otherways be done, to accomplish it by main force of arms, if they had any pity . . ."[10]

Margaret attempted his rescue, and supported by Arran, Argyll, Archbishop Beaton and the Earl of Moray, she marched from Stirling towards Edinburgh. Angus, with the lords of his party and a large force of townsmen of Edinburgh, marched out to meet her, bringing the King with him. Outfaced, and "fearing if they joined in battle the person of their Prince might be endangered", Margaret's army turned tail, and she and her adherents scattered, Margaret and Moray into Moray, Arran and Argyll to the West, Beaton to his residence at Dunfermline. Angus remained master of the country and the King, and returned to Edinburgh confident that his position was secured. Once again the King was forced to write a letter, this time to Beaton, commanding him to resign the Great Seal. Beaton provided a public illustration of the reality of the situation by sending it not to the King, but directly to Angus; this was a gesture which James probably misunderstood, for he always viewed Beaton with suspicion and dislike.

James was in despair as the Douglas net closed around him. One by one Angus's relatives were appointed to offices in the King's household. Sir George Douglas became Master of the Household, while Sir David Lindsay lost his appointment, and, as he said himself:

> . . . durst not be seen
> In open Court, for baith my e'en.

Angus's uncle Archibald Douglas of Kilspindie became Treasurer; James Douglas of Drumlanrig became Master of the Wine Cellar; James Douglas of Parkhead became Master of the Larder. For the King there was no getting away from them. Only one member of Angus's immediate family was excluded from a share in the good fortune: Gavin Douglas, who had died of the plague in London in 1522. He was buried in the Savoy Chapel, where there is a monumental brass which commemorates jointly Thomas Halsey, Bishop of Leighlin, and "Gavin Dowglas, natione Scotus, Dunkelley praesul, patria sua exul." (Gavin Douglas, by nationality a Scot, bishop of Dunkeld, an exile from his native land.) In his political life Gavin Douglas shows at a disadvantage. The splenetic, disappointed cleric is a sad reverse side of a great poet. His "King Hart", his "Palice of Honor" and his Scots translation of the Æneid with its original prologue to each book, make better and more creditable reading than his malevolent libels upon Albany.

With the Douglases triumphant in Scotland, a grim little farce was played out on 14th June 1526, when the King was declared of age, and henceforth ruling by his own authority. This made official — since he was now fourteen, the age at which the Kings of Scots legally attained their majority — what Margaret and Arran had attempted to do unofficially when he was twelve. But the second ceremony was if anything even more meaningless than the first; the King had less independence under Angus than under Margaret. And he could hope for no more help either from his mother or from Arran, for in March 1526 Margaret had married, this time undoubtedly "for her plesour", a man who was probably about eight years younger than herself, Henry Stewart, captain of her guard and younger son of Lord Avondale. This was a *mésalliance* by which she forfeited any respect that had been owed to her former position and any prospect of regaining her political influence. Arran inevitably ceased to support her, and came to terms with Angus.

The position of Angus, however, was less secure than it appeared to be for "his greatness instantly procureth him envy." For this reason, and most probably for his too obviously preferential treatment of his own kinsmen, he forfeited the support of the lords who had backed him against Margaret: the Earls of Cassillis and Glencairn, and more dangerously for him, the Earl of Lennox.

John Stewart, third Earl of Lennox, was young and amiable. He was no less factious than most of the other Scottish lords, but he had the charm which distinguished many members of his family, he had a brave and generous nature, and he was generally liked and admired. In him the King found one of the only two men about him that he did not loathe. The other was Douglas of Kilspindie whom James nicknamed "Graysteil" after the hero of a mediaeval romance that he had read. But Kilspindie being a Douglas was one of his gaolers, a man who might be liked but not trusted. Lennox was only loosely associated with them; he showed the King a warmth and sympathy that they did not. Presently he "so framed himself to the King's humours that he (James) delighted alone in his conversation." Then James decided to trust him, and taking Lennox into his confidence, poured out his woes and begged Lennox to free him from the Douglases. Lennox was not without ambition of his own. He saw himself offered an opportunity to supplant Angus, and resolved to "establish himself in his place, and rule the young King alone."[11] He made a chivalrous response to the King's plea, and promised to free him or lose his life in the attempt.

In July Angus held a Justice Ayre, or itinerant court of criminal justice, on the Borders. The King, whom he never dared leave away from his own surveillance, was brought with him. (Incidentally it was probably from Angus's habit of taking the King on Justice Ayres that James acquired the very thorough knowledge of the law for which he was later much respected.) This particular Justice Ayre provided Lennox with the opportunity to arrange a rescue attempt. He made contact with Scott of Buccleuch, a powerful border laird who was involved in a feud with the Homes and the Kers who supported Angus, and signified to Buccleuch the desire of the King to be freed from Angus's control. Buccleuch could look for the King's future gratitude if he could effect his rescue. Accordingly, when Angus was returning from the Border country to Edinburgh he was met near Melrose by a strong force under Buccleuch, who challenged him to battle. During the engagement Lennox stood beside the King's horse, a neutral observer of the contest. Angus was victorious.

Upon consideration, Angus found the behaviour of Lennox highly suspicious. What was neutrality but failure to support him? What did such failure signify but a desire to see him defeated? Lennox realized that the time had come to show his own hand; he left the court, assuring James that where Buccleuch had failed he himself would succeed. He went to Stirling and from there issued a general appeal to the nobility of Scotland to assist in rescuing the King. He received a response which illustrated the unpopularity of Angus. Supported by the Queen and her despised husband, by Archbishop Beaton, Argyll, Moray, Glencairn and his son the Master of Kilmaurs, Cassillis, Home and Ruthven, he marched towards Edinburgh. Angus prepared a third time to defend his possession of the King, supported by his Douglas kinsmen and "dependers" — an army with fewer names but greater numbers.

On the morning of 4th September, when Angus marched out of Edinburgh, he commanded his brother Sir George Douglas to follow as quickly as he could, bringing the King. James attempted to weaken the Douglas force by division. He "retarded them in some measure, by pretending himself not well . . . and upon the way would often turn aside to ease nature, as if he had been troubled with a looseness." At last Sir George lost his temper. "Sir," he exclaimed,

"Rather than our enemies should take you from us, we will lay hold on your body; and, if it be rent in pieces, we will be sure to take one part of it."[12] The King neither forgot nor forgave those words. If he had hated the Douglases before their ambition had been given such brutal expression, he hated them doubly afterwards.

The battle had been joined near Linlithgow, and when Sir George's force approached the fortune of the day was already with Angus. The King, overwrought with fury and desperately anxious for Lennox, who during the last months had been his only friend and for whom he had latterly felt a "magnetical affection", begged a member of his household, Sir Andrew Wood of Largo, to find out what had happened to Lennox, and make sure that if he were captured he came to no harm. Wood found him already dead, apparently murdered after he had surrendered. Beside his body was the Earl of Arran, who lamented him with the words "The hardiest, stoutest (i.e. bravest) and wisest man that ever Scotland saw lies here slain this day" — a handsome if exaggerated tribute.

The victory went to Angus. He had, however, some losses to balance against it. The murder of Lennox caused Arran's fluid mind to turn against Angus once again, which left Angus's administration without the support of a single member of the greater nobility. Nonetheless, Angus had come off best in three military engagements, and for the present his enemies did not incline to a fourth attempt at his overthrow, even with their conjoint forces. Their defeat at Linlithgow had been serious. It was reported that after the battle Margaret herself "gaed vagrant", no one knew where; and Archbishop Beaton, who also fled in disguise, "turned a true pastor, and in shepherd's weeds kept sheep upon some hill."

Angus brought the King in triumph to Stirling, and this was not the end of his humiliations: he was forced to witness the despoiling of Dunfermline Abbey and St Andrew's

Castle, Angus's reprisal against Archbishop Beaton for attempting the King's rescue. Then followed disciplinary measures against those lords who had taken up arms on the King's behalf. Some of them "compounded for sums of money", others formally came to terms with Angus; none, however, joined his administration. It was a profound humiliation to the King that he remained the captive of a subject, unable to extend his protection to those who had shown loyalty to him. But possibly the most offensive humiliation that Angus offered the King was to bring him to besiege Edinburgh Castle, which Margaret and her husband, reappearing in Angus's absence, had seized, and in which they attempted to defend themselves. Angus's siege was successful, and he compelled Margaret and her husband to sue for James's mercy, and James to commit Henry Stewart to prison in the castle during his pleasure. James had been offended at his mother's *mésalliance*, and rather jealous of Henry Stewart; Angus's vengeful behaviour served to make him think better both of the marriage and the man. In fact Henry Stewart was not undeserving of the King's better opinion. Though he was ambitious his ambition was not disproportionate. As the penniless younger son of one of the lesser lords he obviously considered that his worldly aspirations had been amply fulfilled by marriage to the dowager Queen. He never aspired to obtain, through her, control or even influence over the King. He served the King loyally, and handled the imperious and emotional Margaret with far greater tact and patience than Angus had done. If he had been completely faithful to her, or had resisted completely the temptations of her wealth, he would have been almost inhumanly self-disciplined.

Angus had crushed his opponents and demonstrated the completeness of his victory. Having deprived Archbishop Beaton of the Great Seal some two years previously, he himself officially assumed the chancellorship in August

1527. No one would have imagined that his ascendancy had less than a year to run. Only one pointer indicated that he was vulnerable: that none of his peers was included in his administration. It contained only his own kinsmen, and careerists, some of them very able, from the lesser baronial families.

In the long run, however, what made him most vulnerable of all was the cold hatred of the King, which he had done so much to earn. James had learnt from his mother to dislike and distrust him; his own experiences at Angus's hands had turned those feelings into lasting detestation, which he extended to almost every other member of the house of Douglas. And Angus's treatment of him had another effect, this time one which reversed Margaret's influence: largely since his detested stepfather was the ally of Henry VIII and the chief agent of English influence in Scotland, the English alliance became repugnant to James V, and the ill opinion of Albany and of France which Margaret had instilled in 1524 and Roger Radcliffe had endeavoured to increase, was reversed. James came to appreciate the loyalty of Albany at its proper value, and to set upon the auld alliance a far higher value than it merited. These changes of heart came about gradually, and perhaps almost unconsciously, in the course of Angus's ascendancy. In 1527 what was uppermost in James's mind was loathing of Angus, and determination to escape from his control; but, as Angus had learnt patience in exile, so James learnt it in captivity. He realized that after three defeats he could look for no more armed help from Angus's opponents. His escape must be of his own devising.

Angus was aware of James's hatred; he could scarcely be otherwise after the King had made three attempts to escape from him. If he had been in ignorance that James himself was the prime mover of the rescue attempts he would have learnt the truth from the Earl of Cassillis, who, when he faced the disciplinary measures which followed the battle of Linlithgow, produced a letter from the King appealing for help against Angus. However, Angus attempted to mitigate the King's animosity by spoiling him, and, within the limits of imprisonment, allowing him every indulgence. The sensible clothes provided for him under Albany's regime were replaced with clothes of peacock splendour: gowns, coats and doublets of cloth of gold, "crammasy sattin" and "armasyn sattin" (i.e. satin from Ormuz in the Persian Gulf). The little caps and hoods which he had worn as a child were replaced by the bonnets trimmed with ostrich plumes which became fashionable in the 1520's. James obviously derived great enjoyment from his altered appearance; throughout his life he spent increasingly on clothes and jewels. His surviving portraits all attest a love of splendour which the mood of the times encouraged; he, and all the other sovereigns of Europe, were portrayed in clothes encrusted with jewels and embroidered with a prodigality of pearls. Angus not only allowed him a splendid wardrobe, but also magnificent weapons. Ever since he was twelve he had insisted on wearing a man-sized sword. Now he acquired new swords, a cross-bow and a hand-culverin, with which he enthusiastically practised shooting. But numerous references to horses, hawks and hounds in the Treasurer's Accounts show that he remained attached to traditional forms of sport as well as experimenting with new ones. Besides being allowed to gratify his personal wants, James was permitted to be generous, which could give him the sensation of a certain freedom of action. He was very royal in his generosity to the unfortunate, such as "ane poor wyf", who received twenty shillings for "the slaughter of ane sowe", and John Pumfray "saddillar", who had "fallen in poverty" and received five pounds.[13] He generously rewarded those who brought him little offerings of fruit or game, and there are many examples of presents given by him to those he favoured. The oddest example, which belongs not to the period of Angus's ascendancy but to the year 1531, is the gift of a two handed sword to his Master Cook.[14] Most of his presents were more obviously appropriate.

Fine clothes and weapons, opportunities for sport and the means to be generous were not sufficient to make James's situation tolerable. Angus provided other entertainments, which some observers considered that he offered with more sinister motive than that of winning a more favourable opinion from the King, or distracting him from making trouble. Sir David Lindsay recorded some of them. Though he himself had been driven from court he knew what went on there, presumably from his wife Janet Douglas, who was sempstress to the King, and kept her appointment for the reason made obvious by her maiden name.

Lindsay describes the King playing cards with the young men about the court, the officers of his English guard and the "dependers" of Angus;

> Methought it was a piteous thing,
> To see that fair, young, tender King,
> Of whom these gallants stood no awe,
> To play with him, pluck at the craw.
> They became rich, I you assure,
> But ay the Prince remainit pure.*[15]

That James was a consistent loser is supported by the Treasurer's Accounts. Perhaps the frequency with which he was provided with sums for card-playing, varying between ten shillings and forty pounds, carries the suggestion that he was as frequently "plucked". But gambling remained a distraction for him, and never assumed obsessional proportions. Angus would not have objected if it had. Neither did he object that James's entourage saw to his sexual initiation. Lindsay, whose wife must have heard the young courtiers talking to the King about women, rather amusingly renders their conversation:

* poor.

Quoth one 'The De'il stick me with a knife,
But, Sire, I know a maid in Fife,
One of the lustiest wanton lasses
Whereto, Sire – by God's Blood, she passes!'
'Hold thy tongue, brother,' Quoth another
'I know a fairer, by fifteen futher.*
Sire, when ye please to Lithgow pass
There shall ye see a lusty lass.'
'Now trittyl, trattyl, trolylow!'
Quoth the third man, 'Thou doest but mow!
When his grace comes to fair Stirling
There shall he see a day's darling!'
'Sire,' quoth the fourth, 'Take my counsel
And go all to the high bordel.'[16]

Lindsay obviously disapproved of such an example to a
"fair, young, tender King". He himself, "dominated by
a desire for incorruptibility",[17] might perhaps have committed the reverse mistake of forcing upon the King an
intolerably high standard. But in what shocked him most
he was rightly shocked: that the King's education was
totally abandoned. As he said:

Imprudently, like witless fools
They took that young Prince from the schools.

Lindsay himself, contemporary observers and later historians realized that the policy of Angus and his kinsmen
was deliberately to encourage the King in precocious debauchery for their own ends. Buchanan wrote that "those
who had the instruction of his youth made him more in-
clinable to women, because by that means they hoped to
have him longer under their tuition." More than that.
Angus perhaps hoped that an inadequate education and
habitual debauchery would make the King a *roi fainéant*,
uninterested in taking over the government of his kingdom
and unequipped to do so. The King's maturity was a future

* further.

threat to Angus's tenure of power; and Angus was both ambitious enough and irresponsible enough to desire to neutralize the threat. If that was his intention, however, it was frustrated. Though James's formal education was unimpressive by comparison with that of other renaissance princes, his intelligence was sharp, and in all probability it functioned the more keenly and precociously as a result of his experiences during the ascendancy of Angus. Between the ages of twelve and sixteen he became remarkably self-reliant. He learnt that whatever he wished to attain he himself must wrest from circumstances, by guile when his position was weak, by force when it was strong. As far as his attitudes to other people were concerned, he had always felt affection for his mother, and he had briefly felt it for the Earl of Lennox; but the negative emotion of hatred for Angus far outweighed any positive emotion that he felt for anyone. From the opponents of Angus he did not expect loyalty without self-interest; perhaps his expectation of loyalty was too little to provide inspiration for it. By the time he reached his sixteenth birthday in the spring of 1528 he was self-absorbed, cold hearted and without illusions – or, as Buchanan later described him, "naturally suspicious." But he had sufficient maturity to be both determined to achieve his liberty and confident of his ability to retain and use it.

The King's plan for his escape had its origin in an oversight on the part of Angus. With the over-confidence that grew upon the success he had enjoyed, Angus became careless. Every royal castle had been "seized on by and garrisoned with his friends and followers", with the exception of Margaret's dower castle of Stirling. Perhaps the influence of the Queen had become so negligible since her third marriage that he considered the garrisoning of Stirling more trouble and expense than it was worth – the more so as Margaret herself had not been to Stirling since the battle of Linlithgow. The castle "only haunted by some of her poorest and meanest servants, was neglected"; yet it was one of the strongest fortresses in Scotland. James wrote to his mother and her husband – now at liberty again – and requested them to exchange Stirling Castle for the castle of Methven near Perth. Henry Stewart, upon the King's securing his freedom, would receive the title of Lord Methven. They agreed, and the King wrote summoning Angus's opponents to meet him at Stirling.

Lindsay of Pitscottie, a historian who can be relied upon for the most vivid version of any incident if not for the most accurate one, included in his History a detailed account of the King's escape. It is a story which has been frequently retold. James, who at this time was held by the Douglases at Falkland, found an opportunity of escape when, simultaneously, Sir George Douglas left him to go to St Andrews on business, Kilspindie rode off to visit his mistress in Dundee, and some family matter took Angus to visit his kindred at Lochleven. James Douglas of Parkhead was left in charge of the King. Parkhead did not behave particularly unintelligently, but he was outmanoeuvred by the King's cunning.

The King announced his intention to go hunting, and sent for the Laird of Fernie, the forester of Falkland, whom he ordered to tell the local tenantry to assemble early "and come to Falkland wood at seven hours, for he was determined that he would slay a fat buck or two for his pleasure." Parkhead, of course, would be going with the hunting party, so the King suggested to him that, as it was proposed to make an early start, he and Parkhead should both go early to bed. He then sent for his supper, "drank to James Douglas . . . and bade him be tymmous." (i.e. get up early). "When the watch was set and all things was at quietness", the King got up again, dressed himself in the coat, hose, cloak and bonnet which he had borrowed from one of his Yeomen of the Stable, and slipped out of the palace and into the stables unrecognized. When he left Falkland he took with him two servants whose names are given as Jockie Hairt and Zacharie Harcar, and they rode hard for Stirling where, as prearranged, the King was expected. The castle gates of Stirling were locked behind him, the portcullis was lowered, and the King went to bed to sleep off the exhaustion of the night's ride.

Meanwhile, Sir George Douglas returned to Falkland towards midnight. He enquired what the King – who evidently kept late hours often enough – was doing. He was told that the King had gone to bed. Sir George went to bed himself, only to be woken at sunrise by one Peter Carmichael, Baillie of Abernethy, asking him if he knew where the King was. Sir George replied "He is in his chamber sleeping", to which Carmichael dramatically answered "Nay – he is past the Bridge of Stirling!"

Turmoil ensued. The door of the King's bedchamber was broken open and the bed found empty. Sir George shouted "Fy! Treason!" Someone suggested that the King had "passed to Ballenbriech to a gentlewoman", but others were convinced that the truth was he had gone to Stirling. In the end Angus and Kilspindie were hastily sent for, and they, with Sir George and Parkhead, rode to Stirling to be greeted as they approached the town by a herald with a proclamation forbidding them to approach within six miles of the King's person.

Unfortunately doubts have been cast on Pitscottie's dramatic story because some entries in the Exchequer Rolls suggest that the King's escape was made not from Falkland but from Edinburgh.[18] On the other hand, Pitscottie who came from Fife himself, obtained much of the information for his History from the Laird of Fernie, the forester of Falkland, who according to his account played a small part in the King's escape. The reader is free to believe whichever version he prefers. But whether James escaped from Edinburgh or Falkland, it is certain that he practised some sort of deception upon his gaolers, sometime between 27th and 30th May, and slipped away from them undetected to reappear at Stirling, whence he issued his proclamation forbidding the Douglases to approach him.

Angus realised that he was defeated, for the King had been joined at Stirling by the Earls of Moray, Argyll, Arran, Eglinton, Bothwell, Montrose, Rothes and Marischal, and the Lords Maxwell and Home*, "some of them men not habitually involved in public affairs but evidently prepared to rally to the Sovereign in this crisis";[19] prepared at any rate to rally against a family which had incurred as much envy and emnity as the Douglases. It was futile for Angus to attempt the recapture of the King from so strong a coalition; he withdrew to his castle of Tantallon on the coast of East Lothian, to consider not recovery of power but self preservation. The King, less than two months after his sixteenth birthday, was master of himself and near to attaining the mastery of his kingdom.

This is George 4th Lord Home, younger brother of Alexander 3rd Lord Home and of William his brother executed by Albany in 1516.

Chapter Four

KING OF SCOTS

Now, potent Prince, I say to thee,
I thank the Holy Trinity,
That I have lived to see this day
That all that world* is went away,
And thou to no man art subjected . . .
Sir David Lindsay "The Complaint of Sir David
Lindsay."

JAMES V was a free king at the beginning of June 1528, but his personal rule began ingloriously with several months protracted failure to rid himself of the unwelcome presence of the Douglases in Scotland.

In July James and his supporters occupied Edinburgh. Angus was commanded to retire north of the Spey, and Sir George Douglas and Douglas of Kilspindie to surrender themselves to be "warded" in Edinburgh Castle as sureties for his good behaviour. These commands were ignored, and the Douglases were therefore summoned to appear before the Estates, which were to meet on 3rd September, and hear sentence passed against them. All this time the King and his supporters feared an attempted counter-coup. The King, in residence at Holyrood, was heavily guarded. Possibly he rather enjoyed the atmosphere of tension, for he took his turn at commanding the guard, and staying up all night wearing armour. On other nights he had Sir James Hamilton of Finnart to sleep with him. His sudden partiality for Finnart was surprising, as Finnart was generally believed to be the man who had murdered the Earl of

* i.e. the Douglases.

75

Lennox after the battle of Linlithgow. Either the King did not believe this, or, having taken a liking to Finnart, persuaded himself that he did not believe it. He certainly could not have been ignorant of it, for one of Lennox's servants had followed Finnart to Holyrood, entered the palace and waylaid him in a dark passageway, where he attacked him and left him for dead, bleeding from many stab wounds. However, the alarm was raised, the main gates of the palace locked, and everyone within the great courtyard was searched for evidence of the crime. Lennox's servant was revealed as Finnart's assailant by the bloody dagger which he was still holding. He was immediately seized and imprisoned. Though Finnart recovered from his wounds his attacker was publicly tortured to death in Edinburgh for the attempted murder. He was "carried up and down the city, and every part of his naked body was nipped with iron pincers red hot," wrote Buchanan, who also recorded the stoicism with which he bore this appalling treatment. His last words were that his right hand, which was cut off, "was punished less than it deserved" for failing to slay his master's murderer – a remarkable testimony to Lennox's good qualities as a master, since the servant, who had been a groom, was of too low a status for the blood feud to be obligatory upon him.

According to Lindsay of Pitscottie, Finnart was "a bloody butcher, ever thirsting for blood", a description which seems to have been justified, since he was known to have been embroiled in more than one murder, besides that of Lennox. Furthermore, after the battle of Linlithgow he gave all his prisoners "his mark" – a swordcut across the face – for no better reason than his pleasure. He was probably the most ill-reputed man of his generation, unpopular and generally feared. But he had spent some years in France, where he had acquired taste and education. The degree to which he enjoyed the King's favour fluctuated over the years, but for the time being he was highly favoured.

He was known as the King's "minion", and envy added to his already considerable unpopularity.

On the subject of James's relations with Finnart, only a twentieth century historian remarked that "scandalous reports concerning the Scottish King and his 'minion' Sir James Hamilton were couched in the crudest terms",[1] but no scandalous report was quoted in support of this statement. This appears to be the only incidence of any suggestion that the King's relations with Finnart were homosexual, and indeed, in the case of such a tireless pursuer of women as James V, it would surely be mistaken to suppose that 'minion' is a synonym for 'lover'. In the courtly society of the fifteenth century, and until and beyond the time of James V, friendship as well as love has been described as a matter of "finely made up forms": "two friends dress in the same way, share the same room or the same bed, and call one another by the name of 'mignon'. It is good form for the prince to have his minion"[2] which did not save the person in question from being almost inevitably an object of unpopularity, and often enough a scapegoat for the prince's failures or unpopular actions. It is in this context that the relations of James V with Hamilton of Finnart and later, in particular, with Oliver Sinclair, should be understood. These minions provided the nearest approximation to friends that a man without equals could ever have.

At the beginning of September the Estates duly met and passed sentence of death and forfeiture upon Angus, Sir George Douglas and Douglas of Kilspindie, who prudently did not appear in accordance with the summons. It was strong evidence of the intensity of James's resentment against the Douglases that not even Kilspindie, whom he had liked, was excluded from the sentence of death. The three Douglases were declared guilty of treason in "holding of our sovereign lord's person against his will continually by the space of two years . . . and in exposing of his person to battle, he being of tender age, for the which causes they have forfeited their lives, lands and goods to remain with our sovereign lord and his successors in time to come."[3] The forfeited lands were to be divided among the most favoured of the King's adherents: the Earls of Arran, Argyll and Bothwell, Lord Maxwell, the Laird of Buccleuch, and Hamilton of Finnart.

Besides rewarding those who had supported him following his escape, James paid his other debts of gratitude. Henry Stewart was created Lord Methven, and appointed Master of the Ordnance, "for the love the King bears to his dearest mother." Sir David Lindsay – after he had written two poems to remind the King of his former service and his deserts – was made Snowdon Herald. The nature of his appointment is probably explained by the likelihood of his having been employed as a pursuivant during the ascendancy of Angus, after he had lost his position in the household. At this period the office of Lord Lyon King of Arms had been put into commission, and the four heralds Snowdon, Marchmont, Ross and Ilay were acting jointly on behalf of the Lyon King of Arms. Lindsay later became Lyon Depute, but it was not until 1542, the last year of the reign, that he was formally appointed Lord Lyon King of Arms.

As far as government posts were concerned, the Lord Chancellorship went to the King's erstwhile tutor Gavin Dunbar, who since 1524 had been Archbishop of Glasgow. George Buchanan described him as "a good and learned man, but some thought him a little defective in politics." In fact he proved to be not in the least defective. The opinion of "some" was probably based on the contrasting reputations of himself and the previous ecclesiastic who had held office as Chancellor, Archbishop Beaton, and the contrasting reputations of their families. Gavin Dunbar and his uncle and namesake the Bishop of Aberdeen both had the reputations of good churchmen and men of holy lives; while

Archbishop Beaton was essentially a worldly prelate and a politician, as also was his nephew, David Beaton, Abbot of Arbroath, who became James V's principal adviser in the later years of the reign. However, though the younger Beaton came to enjoy James's trust and favour, the elder could never convince the King that he deserved very much of either. James suspected the Archbishop of treasonable intercourse with England, and declared that he had enriched himself during his chancellorship at the expense of the crown. He preferred the trustworthiness and affection that Gavin Dunbar had shown him in the past to the claims of Archbishop Beaton's greater political experience.

While James rewarded his friends he wisely did not discard certain members of Angus's administration: those careerists whose loyalty was rather to the central government than to the personage who happened to be in power. Robert Barton, a ship owner of Leith and a member of the famous sea-faring family which had produced James IV's admiral Sir Andrew Barton, was retained as Comptroller and subsequently appointed Treasurer. He had first held office as Comptroller under Albany, and then Gavin Douglas had described him as "a very pirate and sea-reiver", but the Douglas administration had subsequently found his services valuable, and his ability continued to be valued by James V. Sir Adam Otterburn of Redhall continued in office as Lord Advocate, and the King employed him also as an ambassador. Angus's Secretary of State, Sir Thomas Erskine of Haltoun was also retained, and served the King both as Secretary and on occasion as an ambassador.

At the outset of his personal rule James therefore had the good fortune to enjoy the loyalty of the nobility, whose support Angus had forfeited, and the wisdom to secure that of those experienced officials on whom Angus had latterly relied.

An act of forfeiture and the reorganisation of the government did not, however, solve the problem presented by the continued presence in Scotland of Angus and his kinsmen. Angus put Tantallon Castle in a state of defence and prepared to resist the sentence passed against them. The King proceeded to military action which proved a humiliating failure. To besiege Tantallon James borrowed "brass guns and powder" from the castle of Dunbar, which was held for the Duke of Albany as part of his patrimony by his deputy, Gonzolles, who continued to hold it until Albany's death in 1536. The siege was unsuccessful, and much to James's fury the Master of the Artillery, David Falconar, was killed after the royal troops had already begun to withdraw. "His death did so enrage the young King, who was incensed enough before, that he solemnly swore in his passion, that as long as he lived, the Douglases should never have the sentence of their banishment revoked."[4] The first necessity, however, was to implement the sentence. After his own failure, James entrusted further military action against the Douglases to the Earl of Argyll, whose greater experience achieved quick results. In November Angus agreed to surrender Tantallon to the King, and he and his kinsmen withdrew to England.

Henry VIII received his erstwhile brother-in-law and supporter favourably, but as he was eager to maintain peace with Scotland he did not make more than a formal protest against Angus's exile. He had begun his long struggle to obtain divorce from Catherine of Aragon, and anticipating trouble with the Emperor, Catherine's nephew, he had no wish to risk a northern war. Accordingly a five years' peace was negotiated between England and Scotland, and ratified at Berwick on 14th December. By the terms of this peace Angus was permitted to remain at the English court, on condition of which his sentence of death was remitted. It was from the signing of this peace that James became completely the master of his kingdom.

His first concern was for the enforcement of law and order. Having been himself the victim of the lawlessness of

Angus, his desire to stamp out lawlessness was vehement and personal. His first efforts were, in the words of Buchanan, "eager and over violent."

Even before he had rid himself of the Douglases he had turned his attention to the enforcement of order. Until the Douglas problem was solved he could do nothing to reduce the Borders to obedience, so accordingly he began with the Highlands where the depredations committed by the Clan Chattan against their neighbours seemed to demand a desperate remedy. The remedy which the young King attempted to provide was savage. On 10th November 1528 he issued "Letters of Fire and Sword" to his half brother James Earl of Moray "our lieutenant general in the north parts of our realm" and to the Earls of Sutherland and Caithness, Lord Forbes, Lord Fraser, and others, by which they were commanded to exterminate the Clan Chattan, without mercy, sparing only priests, women and children. But, "because it were inhumanity to put hands in the blood of women and bairns", these were to be deported and set ashore on the coasts of Shetland and Norway.[5] Fortunately there is some doubt that this order, which had in itself a sufficient appearance of inhumanity, was ever carried out.

The withdrawal of the Douglases to England enabled James to set about the enforcement of orderly living on the Borders. In the early months of 1529 he prepared a large scale expedition. Since the approach of a force of 8,000 men to the Border could not do other than cause alarm in England, James wrote to Henry VIII, signifying his intention: ". . . at this time we are in travel toward our borders, to put good order and rule upon them, and to staunch the thefts and robberies committed by thieves and traitors upon the same. And as our business takes effect, we shall advertise you."[6] Upon this occasion it took effect in the capture and execution of two notorious freebooters, Adam Scott of Tushielaw and Piers Cockburn of Henderland, whose deaths, it was hoped and expected, would act as a deterrent to the activities of others.

The execution of Cockburn of Henderland inspired one of the most powerful of the Border Ballads, the "Lament of the Border Widow", which purports to be the lamentation uttered by Henderland's widow herself:

> My love he built me a bonny bower
> And clad it a' wi' lilye flower;
> A brawer* bower ye ne'er did see
> Than my true love he built for me.
>
> There came a man by middle day,
> He spied his sport and went away,
> And brought the King that very night,
> Who brake my bower and slew my knight.
>
> He slew my knight, to me sae dear;
> He slew my knight, and poin'd his gear;
> My servants all for life did flee
> And left me in extremitie . . .

But those whom Henderland himself had terrorized and bereaved could have spoken with a similar anguish.

For the lawlessness of the Borders – a condition inherent but latterly much increased – James was inclined to blame Angus, as he blamed him for so much else. In letters of credence for an envoy whom he sent to England shortly following his escape, James had written:

"And howbeit the said Earl (Angus) being our chancellor, warden of our east and middle marches, and lieutenant of the same, procured divers raids to be made upon the broken men of our realm, he used our authority not against them, but against our barons and others our lieges, that would not enter in bands of manrent to him, to be so stark of power that we should not be able to reign as his prince, or have dominion above him or our lieges."[7] The "bands of manrent" to which the King referred have been succinctly

* finer.

defined as "feudal covenants . . . compelling the parties to defend each other against the effects of their mutual transgressions."[8]

James particularly suspected the dealings of Angus with the Armstrong family, which enjoyed a degree of independence so great that one of its most powerful members, John Armstrong Laird of Gilnockie, was reputed to have boasted that he acknowledged the authority neither of the King of England nor of the King of Scots. He maintained himself in lavish state by levying "black mail" upon the inhabitants of the countryside surrounding his hold in Liddesdale. It may be added that in the ballad concerning his fate he is made to declare that he had never injured or terrorized any Scot, but had preyed only upon the English. Whether or not this was true, it was intolerable to James that such a degree of independence should be allowed to any subject. In March 1530 he made a second expedition to the Borders, with the specific intention of breaking the power of the Armstrongs.

The King's visit had the appearance of a large scale hunting expedition, and when he approached the Liddesdale district Gilnockie was "enticed by the King's officers" to come and meet him. The meeting took place at Carlinrigg, about ten miles from Hawick. Gilnockie's following numbered forty-eight, and he himself came dressed in such splendour and adorned with such impressive jewels that the King remarked as he approached "What wants that knave that a King should have?", and ironically "moved his bonnet to him". Gilnockie, however, had little awareness of fine shades of meaning and supposed that he was being received with honour – until he and his followers were seized and made prisoner. According to the ballad "Johnie Armstrong", Gilnockie pleaded desperately for his life, making the King extravagant promises of tribute in money and in kind. But James remained adamant, replying to each promise and entreaty

83

> Away, away, thou traitor strang,
> Out of my sight soon mayest thou be
> I granted never a traitor's life,
> And now I'll not begin with thee.

James's "never" did not reach back over a very long period, but he had begun as he intended to go on. At last Gilnockie realized that entreaties were useless, and submitted himself to his fate with dignity, saying as he was led to his death

> To seek hot water beneath cold ice
> Surely it is a great follie.
> I have asked grace at a graceless face
> And there is none for my men and me.*

The unknown author of the verse that speaks for Gilnockie sketched the King, or at least the aspect of him displayed by that incident, with sharp realism. Cold and graceless or, as we should say ruthless, indeed Gilnockie and his followers found the King, as Tushielaw and Henderland, and possibly a proportion of the Clan Chattan had previously found him. Popular tradition, which made Gilnockie into a Robin Hood figure who robbed the rich and gave to the poor, related that he and his forty-eight followers were hanged on growing trees, which thereafter withered and died. Doubtless the sympathy with which he was remembered had its origin not in any chivalrous qualities that he may have possessed, but in the unsavoury manner in which he was brought to his death.

Of the Border Ballads which deal with historical events it has been said truly enough that they do not record "actual historical happenings, but highly stylized *versions* of actual happenings."[9] No doubt "Johnie Armstrong" presents a highly stylized version of James V's dealings with Gilnockie; but no contrary evidence exists to cast doubt upon the actual facts of the happening. It may well have approximated as nearly to the narrative of the ballad as the shape-

---

* For the full text of the ballad, see Appendix A.

lessness of events ever comes to the shapeliness of poetry.
Pitcairn's Ancient Criminal Trials at least preserves the
record that John Armstrong, "alias Black Jok" and his
brother Thomas Armstrong, Laird of Mangerton, were
hanged on 1st April, 1530.[10]

As a result of the example made of Cockburn of Henderland, Scott of Tushielaw and the Armstrongs, and of the
imprisonment of several of the powerful border lairds, the
Borders were quietened. It may not have been a contented
quiet, but at least "overt disaffection was extinguished for
the rest of the reign."[11] The King's achievement impressed
his contemporaries; it impressed them even further that
he was able to keep vast flocks of sheep unmolested in
Ettrick Forest as safe as if they had been "within the
bounds of Fife."

The King's dealings with the Highlands and Isles from
1529 onwards had a more conciliatory appearance. During
the King's minority and under Angus's regime the keeping
of order in the Western Highlands and the Isles had been
entrusted to the third Earl of Argyll, who died in 1529.
James was deeply suspicious of the immense influence
wielded by his family, the Campbells, over so large an
area; and, when Colin, fourth Earl of Argyll succeeded his
father, James took the opportunity to reduce his official
powers. Argyll wrote to the Council in 1531, requesting
that the King should grant him a Commission of Lieuten-
andry over the South Isles, an appointment which his
father had held, "because I and my friends has as great
experience in the daunting of the Isles . . . as any others of
the realm, and specially for the destruction of them inobedient to the King's grace . . ."[12] James, however, was
more disposed to listen to the island chief Alexander
MacDonald of Islay, Argyll's enemy, who argued that
Argyll's policy was to make trouble in the Isles, so that
while he could be seen dutifully to daunt and destroy the
"inobedient", he himself was the person who profited by

their fall and stood to acquire by conquest or reward their lands and possessions. It was Alexander MacDonald who received the commission to keep the South Isles in obedience and see that the crown tenants there paid their rents. Argyll was briefly imprisoned in 1531, and remained out of favour for several years. Nevertheless, as a great landowner and the chief of a large clan, he was always a power to be reckoned with.

The King's policy could be represented as one of conciliation towards the Isles, shown by the employment of an island chief, instead of a policy merely of "daunting of the Isles"; or it could be represented as a policy of deliberate undermining of the power of the Campbells by the employment of Alexander MacDonald in the place of Argyll. Considering that James seldom showed a conciliatory spirit under any circumstances, and that a deep distrust of the greater nobility had been implanted in him by his experiences at the hands of the Douglases, it seems probable that the reduction of the power of the Campbells was the true motive of his policy.

The power of the Campbells in the Western Highlands and the Isles was equalled by that of the Gordons, Earls of Huntly, in the North. George, fourth Earl of Huntly, was slightly younger than the King. He had succeeded to his earldom in 1524 at the age of ten, and had been the ward of Angus. Consequently he and the King had had the opportunity to become closely acquainted under circumstances tending to the development of mutual sympathy; and the King came to have a trust and liking for him that he had for no other member of the greater nobility. Since he enjoyed the King's friendship the powers of Huntly's family were left undiminished; James felt that he could be confident they would be used in the interests of the crown.

But in too many instances James's dealings with his nobility were high handed and unwise. Possibly, exalted by his early and apparently easy successes, he did not stop to consider the extent to which he was in fact dependent upon retaining the goodwill of his most powerful subjects. To permit the development of a strong opposition party could prove fatal; such a party had brought about the downfall and murder of James III. James IV had learnt the lesson of his father's fate, and his policy towards his nobles had been both to conciliate and to divide them. At the same time, by the power and attraction of his personality he had been able to inspire their loyalty. James V had not had the advantage of a terrible object lesson such as his father had received; neither did he learn the lessons of the past through considering the achievements and failures of his immediate ancestors. He relied too much upon the direct, and indeed tactless, use of his authority, and upon his very considerable powers of intimidation, in the possession of which he resembled his uncle, Henry VIII.

In the early years of the King's personal rule short spells of imprisonment were endured by several lords besides Argyll. The Earls of Bothwell and Moray, Lords Home and Maxwell, and the border lairds of Johnston, Polwarth, Ferniherst and Buccleuch were all imprisoned at one time and another between 1529 and 1531. Moray and Maxwell were only briefly out of favour and they, while retaining a certain sense of grievance, remained loyal to the King. Bothwell, however, was seriously disaffected, and considered transferring his allegiance to the King of England. In December 1531 he secretly met the Earl of Northumberland, to whom he explained the causes of his resentment against James V, which were "the giving of his lands to the Carres of Teviotdale; the keeping of him half a year in prison, and seeking to apprehend him and his colleagues, that he might lead them to execution." Northumberland wrote to Henry VIII that Bothwell ". . . doth say, remembering the banishment of the Earl of Anguisse (Angus), the wrongful disinheriting of the Earl of Crawford, the sore imprisonment of the Earl of Argyll, the little estimation of the Earl Murray (Moray) and the Lord Maxwell, the simple regarding of Sir James Hamilton for his good and painful services (this is probably Sir James Hamilton of Kincavel, Sheriff of Linlithgow), he puts no doubt with his own power and the Earl of Anguisse's seeing all these nobles' hearts afore expressed be withdrawn from the King of Scots, to crown your grace in the town of Edinburgh within brief time."[13]

Apparently Bothwell supposed that with Henry as King "the realm of Scotland shall be brought into good state again, and not the nobles thereof be kept down as they are in thralldom, but to be set up as they have been before"; a supposition which Henry's systematic reduction of the independence of the English nobility makes extremely doubtful. Bothwell's representation of the disaffection produced by James's high handed treatment of his nobility sounds sensational, but it was probably exaggerated, for no action followed the meeting of Bothwell and Northumberland. Nonetheless, it was illustrative of the extent to which James's popularity with his lords had been eroded since they had rallied to him in June 1528. But whatever dissatisfaction or unease they felt, only Angus, whose fortunes in Scotland seemed ruined beyond hope of recovery, actually took the action which Bothwell supposed himself not alone in contemplating; an agreement exists by which Angus promised Henry VIII to "make unto us the oath of allegiance, and recognize us as supreme Lord of Scotland, and as his prince and sovereign."[14]

* * *

Although James applied himself with a vigour which Buchanan seems to have been justified in describing as "eager and over-violent" to the task of reducing his kingdom to order and his nobility to obedience, he did not at the same time deny himself pleasures and recreations.

In the summer of 1530 he went on a progress to the

Highlands, in the course of which he was magnificently entertained by the Earl of Atholl. James brought with him Queen Margaret and the Papal Ambassador. They were lodged in a rustic palace "built in the midst of a fair meadow, of green timber, woven about with birches that were green both under and above". The appearance and furnishing of this summer palace were minutely described by Lindsay of Pitscottie: the palace had a great round tower at each corner, a tower on either side of its entrance, a moat, a drawbridge, and "a great portcullis of timber which fell down in the manner of a barrier." Inside "the floor was laid with green turfs" and strewed "with rushes, meadow-sweet and flowers." Every luxury to which the King was accustomed was provided: ". . . this palace was well roofed and within was hung with fine tapestries and silken arrases, and set with fine glass windows on all sides. So this palace was in all ways as pleasantly decorated with all necessaries pertaining to a prince as if it had been his own royal palace at home." The entertainment was as sumptuous as the surroundings: ". . . this earl caused to be made such provision for the King and his mother and that stranger the ambassador that they had all manner of meats, drinks and delicacies that were to be got at that time in all Scotland either in town or country; that is to say all kinds of drinks, as ale, beer, wine, both white wine and claret, malmsey, muscatel and alicante, hippocras and *aqua vitae*. Furthermore, for the food there was white almond bread and ginger-bread, with various meats: beef, mutton, lamb, rabbits, cranes, swans, wild geese, partridges and plovers, duck, turkeys and peacocks, together with blackcock, moorfowl and capercailzie." All around the palace fishponds had been dug and stocked with "salmon, trout and perch, pike and eels, and all other kinds of delicate fish that could be found in fresh water, and all were ready to be prepared for the banquet." The King "remained in this present wilderness at the hunting for the space of three days and three nights."

And, "I heard say," wrote Pitscottie, "the King at that time, in the bounds of Atholl and Strathearn . . . slew thirty score of harts and hinds, with other small beasts, as roe and roebuck, wolf and fox and wildcats." These three days of banquet and slaughter were reputed to have cost Atholl three thousand pounds.

It was evidently a great source of satisfaction to Pitscottie, in recording Atholl's entertainment of the King, that "this ambassador of the Pope's seeing this great banquet and triumph being made in a wilderness where there was not a town near by twenty miles, thought it a great wonder that such a thing should be in Scotland"; for Scotland, in the estimation of other nations "was but the arse of the world." But the amazement of the ambassador was increased "when the King departed and all men took their leave," for "the highland men set all this fair palace afire, that the King and the ambassador might see it." With the green wood dried out by the summer weather, the palace and all the luxuries it contained blazed to nothing before their eyes – a prodigal gesture on the part of the Earl of Atholl, and a dramatic conclusion to his entertainment.

"Then the ambassador said to the King 'I marvel that you should permit yon fair palace to be burnt, that your Grace has been so well lodged in.' Then the King answered the ambassador and said 'It is the use of our highland men, though they be never so well lodged, to burn their lodging when they depart.' "[15] The dry humour of the King's comment on the habits of the highlanders was perhaps lost upon "that stranger the ambassador."

Entertainment which provided "all necessaries pertaining to a Prince" was not the only kind that James enjoyed. He also sought informal hospitality from his poorer subjects. He had a taste for disguise and adventure, and it was probably in the years following his escape and preceding his marriage that he had most opportunity to indulge it. The stories of his incognito wanderings, which are part of the popular history of Scotland, are very much more reminiscent of folktales than of biographical anecdotes; yet if the stories of his encounters with millers, tinkers and robbers cannot all be claimed as accurately recorded anecdotes, some of them are worth retelling for the sidelights they provide on the King's character. If some of them were mere inventions, they were invented because they seemed characteristic of him.

For example, it is told that on one occasion James was separated from a hunting party which had set out from Falkland Palace. He came to the township of Milnathort, a few miles from Falkland, and there went into the inn, where he found a tinker sitting drinking, and joined him. James mentioned the royal hunt, and the tinker said that he had never seen the King and wished that he could do so. James suggested that they should go out and look for the hunt, which they did, both mounted on James's horse. The tinker asked how, if they came upon the hunting party, he would recognise the King among all his lords. Because, James replied, the King would be the only one among them who would wear his hat. Presently they came upon the hunt, and at sight of the King all swept off their hats and bowed — whereupon the tinker, realizing the identity of his companion, slid off the horse and knelt to the King.

A story with an almost identical conclusion, more frequently retold, describes how Jock Howieson, the miller of Cramond, rescued the King from a party of robbers which attacked him, and afterwards took him home to the mill and washed and bound up his wounds, before escorting him on his way towards Edinburgh. To Jock Howieson James described himself as the Gudeman of Ballengiech, tenant farmer of one of the royal farms. Howieson, invited to Holyrood, was promised a sight of the King, whom he would know by the same means as the tinker. When, in the King's Presence Chamber, they were confronted by a group of courtiers who took off their hats and bowed,

Howieson's reaction was more egalitarian than the tinker's — for it is said that Howieson, who was wearing a cap himself, turned to stare at the King, and exclaimed "Then it must be either you or me, for all but us are bareheaded!" Jock Howieson received his reward for the rescue of the King — the freehold of the royal farm of Braehead — on condition that his descendants should always receive the King's successors whenever they should pass the Bridge of Cramond where the rescue had taken place, and there offer a bowl of water and a towel in memory of the service which Jock Howieson had performed for James V. This ritual was performed by descendants of Jock Howieson, or at any rate by occupiers of Braehead, for George IV in 1822, for Queen Victoria in 1842, for George V in 1927, and for George VI in 1937. While this appears to give one of the traditional anecdotes of James V a basis in fact, it is difficult to avoid the suspicion that the idea which inspired these late performances of the ritual may have originated in the mind of Sir Walter Scott, the producer and director of George IV's highly theatrical visit to Scotland in 1822.

Another tale involving the disguise and revelation of the King is that of his encounter with a Stirlingshire laird, Buchanan of Arnprior. The laird, his stock of provision depleted by the demands of hospitality, attacked a hunting party which passed temptingly close to Arnprior on its way to Stirling with a supply of venison for the King's kitchens. The members of the hunting party resisted Buchanan's men and told them the venison was for the King; whereupon Buchanan replied that while James Stewart might be King of Scotland, Buchanan of Arnprior was King of Kippen — the district surrounding Arnprior. But Buchanan was too close to Stirling for such an arrogant claim to be anything but ridiculous; he was fortunate that the King took him less seriously than he had taken Armstrong of Gilnockie. James rode the two miles or so from Stirling to Arnprior alone and in disguise, and told the guards at the gate to tell Buchanan that the Gudeman of Ballengiech had come to dine with the King of Kippen. Buchanan came out to kneel at the King's feet and ask his pardon; James granted it, and went in to dine on his own venison.

It is interesting to notice that while James would not tolerate Buchanan's styling himself King of Kippen, he allowed one man in Scotland besides himself to use the style of King – Johnny Faa, the King of the Gipsies. Possibly the real or supposed racial difference between the Gipsies and all other subjects of James V was at the basis of this tolerance: the belief that the Gipsies were not Scots but wandering 'Egyptians' scattered like the Jews throughout all lands. The Faas, "Kings and Earls of Little Egypt", claimed the allegiance of the Gipsies of Roxburghshire, Berwickshire and Northumberland, and from the end of the seventeenth century they became more or less settled in the Roxburghshire village of Kirk Yetholm, where they held their court and were crowned with iron crowns made for them by the local blacksmiths. Their dynasty outlasted that of the Stewarts; the last of the Faas, a reigning Queen, died in 1898.

To revert once more to the traditional tales of James V, most of them have certain elements in common besides their folktale ethos. They show the King possessed of a sense of gratitude, of generosity and personal courage, and of a somewhat heartless sense of humour which found amusement in the confusion of others. He obviously derived considerable entertainment from watching the effect upon them of the revelation of his identity, by which he showed himself, especially in the last instance, as a king who could be affable and familiar but might not be trifled with.

Tales of the King's adventures and of his acts of generosity were current in his lifetime, and contributed to the popularity which he long enjoyed among the commons of Scotland. "The Gudeman of Ballengiech" – the identity which he most frequently assumed – came to be almost synonymous for "The King" among them, as the story of

Buchanan of Arnprior suggests. His other nicknames also attest his popularity: "The Reid Tod" (i.e. the Red Fox) and "The King of the Commons". The King was familiar to his people, for he travelled widely in the Lowlands, made numerous expeditions to the Highlands, and was always "easy of access even to the poorest."[16] Possibly, as he wandered among them, he was recognized more frequently than he realized; he was not a man who could have disguised himself easily. With his red hair and white complexion, with his eagle-like profile, and with hands which obviously had never done manual labour, he could not have mingled very unnoticeably in a crowd of country-people, or, on close inspection, have looked very much like the farmer he claimed to be.

It is paradoxical, but perfectly understandable, that the severity of James V was as much contributory to his popularity with the commons as his wanderings and escapades among them. To those who had suffered at the hands of the lawless, and to those who wished only to live their lives without the threat of violence, the King appeared in the guise of a protector. None questioned the deterrent power of savage punishments; that the King saw them enforced was a reassurance to his people. But he did more than that. George Buchanan describes how the King would "sit on horseback, night and day, in the coldest winter, that so he might catch the thieves in their harbours at unawares: and his activity struck such a terror into them, that they abstained from their evil purposes, as if he had been always present among them." That he should sacrifice his own comfort and rest to ensure his people's earned him love and gratitude which were well enough merited.

The dangers to which his taste for adventure and his personal pursuit of malefactors exposed him made the King's advisers anxious that he should secure the succession by marrying and begetting heirs – the more so as they were well aware that not all his night rides were undertaken in the interests of law and order. He would ride by night, sometimes with a few companions but more often alone, to visit one or other of his mistresses, of whom he had several in the years preceding his marriage. Thence came an added reason why he should marry with little delay, for bastards did nothing to secure the succession, and might indeed provide a future threat to it; and the King's mistresses Elizabeth Shaw of Sauchie, Margaret daughter of Lord Erskine, Euphemia daughter of Lord Elphinstone, Elizabeth daughter of Lord Carmichael, and Elizabeth Stewart, all bore him sons. Elizabeth Beaton of Creich bore him a child whose name and sex are unknown.

As the King turned occasionally from courtly to informal entertainment, so occasionally he turned from affairs with daughters of his nobility to informal sexual adventures. Perhaps he found it necessary to reassure himself that women would accept James Stewart the man when he had no more advantages than any other man; for any woman, or almost any woman, would surrender to the King. Memories of such adventures survive in two poems, "The Gaberlunzie Man"* and "The Jolly Beggar", which were so closely associated with the King as to become popularly attributed to his authorship, although linguistically they belong to a later period. Both poems are variations on the same theme. In each instance a man disguised as a beggar makes a conquest of a country girl. In "The Jolly Beggar" he subsequently reveals his identity and provides for the child he has fathered:

> He took the lassie in his arms
>   And gae her kisses three
> And four and twenty hunder merk
>   To pay the nurse's fee;
> He took a wee horn frae his side
>   And blew baith loud and shrill
> And four and twenty belted knights
>   Came skipping owre the hill.

* Gaberlunzie (pronounced Gayberloonie) = a beggar.

And we'll go no more a-roving
A-roving in the night,
Nor sit a sweet maid loving
By coal or candle light.

And he took out his little knife
Loot a' his duddies fa',*
And he was the brawest† gentleman
That was among them a'.
The beggar was a clever loon
And he lap shoulder height
"O ay for siccan quarters
As I got yesternight!
And we'll ay gang a-roving
A-roving in the night,
For then the maids are loving
And stars are shining bright."

This is folk poetry, and so is the more famous poem "Christis Kirk on the Green" which is also traditionally attributed to James V. However, in Scotland until the eighteenth century "People of all stations lived closely to one another. The 'Lands' (tenements) of Edinburgh . . . came right down to the Palace Yetts (i.e. the gates of Holyroodhouse) . . . Many of the great songs of the peasant life are not by peasants but by the gentry who fully understood their ways and feelings."[17] It was not, therefore, illogical to attribute folk poems to the King of the Commons. If "The Gaberlunzie Man" and "The Jolly Beggar" are now recognized as being *about* James V rather than *by* him, the case of "Christis Kirk on the Green", a *genre* poem "like a Breughel Kermesse", is rather different. Nothing stronger than a long tradition connects it with the King, but no conflicting tradition or contrary evidence connects it with any other poet. It is written in a stanza form which has been frequently used for the last six centuries in Scottish poetry, and which appears to originate with the anonymous

* i.e. He cut off all his rags.   † finest.

mediaeval poem "Peblis to the Play", to which a reference is made in the fourth line of the first verse of "Christis Kirk on the Green". It is a stanza form used by Henrysoun, by Robert Fergusson, by Burns and by the contemporary poet Robert Garioch. It is an intricate but flexible form, not too sophisticated for the subject matter of "Christis Kirk on the Green" – the deterioration of a rustic revel into an uproarious free-for-all:

> Was never in Scotland heard nor seen
> Such dancing nor deray*
> Neither in Falkland on the green
> Nor Peebles to the play,
> As was of wooers as I ween
>
> At Christis kirk on a day.
> There came our Kitty washing† clean
> In her new kirtle of gray
>   ull gay
> At Christis kirk on the green.

There follows a charming description of the local girls dressed in their finery:

> To dance the damsellis them dicht‡
> And lasses light of laittis§
> Their gloves were of the raffell‖ richt
> Their shoon were of the straitis¶,
> Their kirtles were of lincoln licht𝕵
> Well pressed with many plaitis**
> They were so nice when men them nicht‡‡
> They squealed like any gaitis§§
>   Full loud
> At Christis kirk on the green.

Tom Lutar the minstrel plays for them, they start to dance, and from that moment the "deray" (disorder) begins.

James V may possibly have written this poem, and evi-

---

* disorder. † washed. ‡ dressed up. § manners. ‖ roe-deer skin. ¶ morocco leather. 𝕵 lincoln green. ** pleats. ‡‡ came near them. §§ goats.

dence that he certainly wrote poetry comes from Sir David Lindsay's poem "The Answer which Sir David Lindsay made to the King's Flyting."

"Flytings" were exchanges of abuse in verse, each one "an accretion of aggressive, vituperative 'tumbling verse' delivered at top speed, but they had to be poetically declaimed"; when done well the result was a "fluent flood-gate of torrential but glittering abuse."[18] To hear the flyting of rival poets was a popular entertainment at the courts of James IV and James V, and was revived again at the court of James VI. It appears from Lindsay's poem that the King challenged him to a flyting, in verses which have not survived. Lindsay replies that though unwilling to abuse his King, he will obey him and write an answer. But in his answer, instead of writing a humorous vituperation, he takes the opportunity to write the King a very forthright homily. James had accused Lindsay of being a sluggard in the pursuit of love; Lindsay accuses James of being over-enthusiastic in the pursuit of it —

> On ladronis for to leap, ye will not let*

He warns him against the evils of excessive self-indulgence and the risks of venereal diseases, and reproaches him for raping a servant maid who had first emptied a brewing vat over his head and then surrendered in the resulting puddle of beer and lees. Lindsay was not expending any pity on "that duddroun" (i.e. that slut), but telling the King that the squalor of the incident brought him discredit:

> Would God the lady that lovit you best
> Had seen you there lie swettering† like twa swine.[19]

The 'lady that lovit you best' was Margaret Erskine, the King's favourite mistress, whom he seriously considered marrying; and had he done so it would not have been a *mésalliance*. Earlier Stewart Kings, Robert II and Robert III,

* You never rest from leaping upon whores.
† wallowing.

had married Scottish noblewomen, and English noble families provided the second, third, fifth and sixth wives of Henry VIII. A royal bride, or a bride from a princely or reigning ducal family was not essential for prestige so much as for political or financial reasons. James might have contented himself with Margaret Erskine had not financial necessity compelled him to enter negotiations for a foreign marriage. He was in an advantageous position, for, as the Emperor and the Kings of England, France and Portugal were married, the King of Scots was the most desirable match for any princess in Europe.

Chapter Five

THE ANCIENT ALLIANCE AND
THE OLD RELIGION – I

... At his marriage made upon the morn ...
There sealit was the confirmation
Of the well keepit ancient alliance
Made betwixt Scotland and the realm of France.
*Sir David Lindsay "The Deploratioun
of the Deith of Quene Magdalene."*

THE poverty of the Crown at the time of James's escape
from the Douglases necessitated that he should find a bride
with a dowry large enough not only to support the dignity
of a Queen but also to recoup his own financial position.
During the minority the revenues of the Crown had been
ruinously depleted. In the reign of James IV the total
ordinary revenue had approached £30,000 *per annum*;
but Albany had been expensive and Margaret extravagant,
and in the financial year 1525-6 the total had scarcely
exceeded £13,000.[1] Angus had not attempted retrench-
ment, or any other means of financial recovery, and by March
1530 James was reduced to borrowing 2,000 merks from
Huntly. A rich marriage seemed to offer the quickest
possibility of remedy; quickest because a certain amount of
preliminary diplomacy had already taken place. Indeed,
the marriage of James V had been under discussion from
the very beginning of his reign and was a matter of some
international importance. Both the balance of power in
Europe and the effect of the spreading Reformation on the
European situation gave alliance with Scotland a potentially
greater value than it had possessed in previous centuries.

James V grew up with the idea that he would marry the Princess Madeleine of France, in accordance with the terms of the Treaty of Rouen; but other possible marriage alliances had been discussed. In 1524–5, during Margaret's brief ascendancy, there had been talk of a marriage between James and Mary of England. Queen Margaret naturally considered this marriage the best that her son could make, but even she did not favour Henry VIII's proposal that James should be sent to England to complete his education. Henry VIII, if he could not use the marriage of James and Mary as the means to secure the custody of James would have preferred at this point to marry Mary to the Emperor. The negotiation between Margaret and Henry accordingly came to nothing. It sufficed, however, to cause anxiety to Albany, whose departure from Scotland did not lessen his concern that the auld alliance should be reaffirmed. François Ier was not at this time prepared to honour the Treaty of Rouen. After his defeat at Pavia he became more concerned to maintain friendly relations with England than to ally himself with Scotland, the lesser power. Albany felt that the auld alliance could be tacitly reaffirmed without upsetting the diplomatic balance sought by François Ier if James were to marry the Duchess of Albany's niece, Catherine de Medici. Catherine, the daughter of Madeleine de la Tour, Albany's sister-in-law, and of Lorenzo de Medici, Duke of Urbino, was an heiress of vast wealth and the ward of Pope Clement VII, her father's kinsman. Albany's proposal, though acceptable to François Ier, did not commend itself to the Pope, who was reluctant to see his ward married in such a distant country as Scotland. He complained that the cost of sending messengers to and from Scotland would be heavier than the cost of the dowry.

English diplomacy took advantage of the Pope's reluctance, for Henry VIII was on his guard to prevent Albany's recovering his influence in Scotland, which might well come about through the marriage of Catherine de Medici to the

King of Scots. Other proposals, however, were made for James's marriage. The deposed King of Denmark, Christian II, offered the choice of his daughters, the Princesses Christina and Dorothea, either with a dowry of 10,000 crowns, in the hope that he would secure Scottish help in regaining his throne which had been usurped by Frederick, Duke of Holstein. The offered dowry was not very large, but the proposal was kept under consideration.

This was the stage which the marriage diplomacy had reached when James escaped from the custody of Angus. At once he sent Sir William Hamilton of Marcniston to France to request the hand of the Princess Madeleine. François put off giving a definite answer by truthfully pointing out that Madeleine was not yet old enough for marriage. James then decided that the Danish marriage was worth considering. He sent Hamilton to the Emperor to discover whether the proposal had his support, since the Danish princesses were his nieces, and the marriage would bring Scotland into alliance with the Empire. This embassy revealed that Charles V set a high value on alliance with Scotland, for he offered James, in preference to a Danish marriage, the hand of his own sister Mary, the widowed Queen of Hungary.

In spite of the coolness shown by François Ier, James preferred the auld alliance to the prospect of an alliance with the Emperor; for Austria and Spain, the centres of Imperial power, were far distant, whereas France, besides being the traditional ally, was a near neighbour. Furthermore, though in the past the auld alliance had proved more politically beneficial to France than to Scotland, it was at least theoretically possible from the Scottish viewpoint to play off France against England, but there was no question that the Empire could be used for this purpose. However, James saw that the Imperial proposal might be used to induce François Ier to honour the Treaty of Rouen as a means of preventing an alliance between Scotland and the Empire. James did not make an immediate approach to the King of France. Instead, on 10th May, 1529, he wrote to Albany – to whom he did not, of course, mention the financial reason for his desire to marry as quickly as possible.

"Nous semble meilleur et plus expédient," he wrote, "vous advertir et faire entendre que sommes grandement pressez (sic) par les Etats de nostre Royaulme et nostre Conseil de praindre alliance et marriage là on il sera trouvé le plus expédient et séant pour nous et le bien publique de nostre Royaulme." He went on to say that it was expedient he should marry not only because the succession was unsecured but also "pour évyter la procréation des batardz lesquelz par cy devant on mys grant trouble en ce Royaulme." He added that he felt it proper to inform Albany that he had received offers of the Emperor's sister or one of his nieces "avec tres grant argent . . ."[2] François, it was implied, might wish to make a counterbid.

The result, if not quite all that James had hoped, was not wholly unsatisfactory. François remained unwilling either to risk alienating Henry VIII or to commit his young and delicate daughter Madeleine to marriage. At that same time he did not wish to see James allied with the Emperor. Accordingly he allowed Albany once more to propose a marriage between James and Catherine de Medici, with the hope that this time the Pope could be induced to consent. Catherine's wealth might well have been sufficient to compensate for the greater prestige of Madeleine's birth. James certainly saw this aspect of the proposal. He did not allow his negotiations with the Emperor to lapse, but, after considering the advantages of the Medici marriage as potentially providing both the necessary dowry and the re-affirmation of the auld alliance, eventually in 1530 he made up his mind, and sent Sir Thomas Erskine of Haltoun to Rome to negotiate his marriage to Catherine.

The unwillingness of the Pope was not the only barrier to the success of Erskine's mission. As before, Henry VIII did not wish to see the auld alliance reaffirmed, or to see his old enemy Albany reappear to trouble him as the uncle of the Queen of Scotland. He therefore prevailed upon François Ier to make a rival proposal for Catherine's hand on behalf of his second son Henri, Duc d'Orléans. It is a futile but intriguing line of speculation to wonder how the course of Scottish history might have been altered if Catherine de Medici had become the Queen of Scotland. Her fate, however, lay in France, and when years later, Mary, Queen of Scots made her well known derogatory reference to Catherine de Medici as "une fille des marchands", she presumably did not know that Catherine had ever been under consideration as a bride for her father.

The Pope preferred the French to the Scottish proposal but he was now well aware of the evil effect that matrimonial disappointments could have on the relations between the papacy and the temporal powers; and, in view of the situation which was developing in England, he was anxious to ensure the maintenance of good relations with James V. Fortunately ". . . Scottish candour in admitting that James's interest was less in Catherine than in her dowry suggested a means to console James for the refusal of his bride . . ."[3]

Sir Thomas Erskine, in his original instructions, had been directed to entrust Albany with the task of requesting from the Pope the renewal of an indult which had been granted to Albany during his own regency, which had permitted him to annex both the temporalities and the spiritualities of vacant prelacies. Obviously an ecclesiastical subsidy — likewise drawn from Scottish sources — would provide a satisfactory means to console the King; but it would have to be a subsidy on a very much larger scale than that suggested by the original instructions to Erskine. Since the ensuring of the obedience and orthodoxy of Scotland in the face of the dangerous example of England was what was uppermost in the Pope's mind, on 9th July 1531 he wrote to the prelates of Scotland asking for their

views on the imposition of a permanent tax of £10,000 a
year to be levied on their prelacies for "the protection and
defence of the realm" – a phrase capable of wide interpretation which adequately conveyed to them what he meant.
For this avowed purpose he actually imposed a tax, known in
Scotland as the "Three Teinds", of one tenth of the income
of all benefices worth more than £20 *per annum*, for three
years; for the imposition of the permanent tax of £10,000
a year, which was known as the "Great Tax", a better
defined purpose had to be found. The purpose suggested
to the Pope was the foundation and endowment of a "College
of Justice", or a body of salaried professional judges, in
Scotland. Of the background to the foundation of the
College of Justice it is necessary to give some explanation.

The efficient administration of civil justice had been a
perennial problem in Scotland, and during the fifteenth
century "various experiments had been made to form and
maintain a supreme court for civil causes." In the reign of
James III judicial sessions of the King's Council had been
held to hear civil causes, and these judicial sessions developed
in the reign of James IV into a "Court of Session" which
was directed to sit during specified terms in the year. Some
members of the Court of Session were designated "Lords
of Council and Session" and others, as now not all were
councillors, were described as "Lords of Session". The
principal difficulty in the way of the efficient working of this
court was to ensure the regular attendance of a large enough
number of its members. The spring session of 1527, during
the ascendancy of Angus, had to be abandoned for lack of
attendance, and some privileged litigants were then commanded to bring their cases to the Justice Ayres, on which
fell the burden of some of the civil as well as the criminal
justice. Before 1528 "the difficulty of maintaining an ade-
quate attendance had induced the authorities to welcome any
magnate who chose to lend his assistance – an intervention,
it is to be feared, rarely offered from disinterested motives."[4]

In 1528 James V, no doubt motivated by his deep-rooted suspicion of the greater nobility, closed the Session to anyone not specifically nominated a member of it. This did nothing to solve the problem of insufficient attendance, especially as the members of the Session were not paid, and possibly not many apart from the greatest nobles could easily bear the expenses of attendance. In 1531 the Chancellor, Archbishop Dunbar, produced a new set of Rules "Anent the Ordering of the Session . . .", which attempted a solution. Thirty-five members were nominated, who were to be the Chancellor himself, fifteen spiritual and thirteen temporal members, with the addition of six government officials as extra members. From this total, fourteen were always to be on duty. But they were still unpaid, and it was obvious that the payment of salaries would be the most effective method of ensuring their attendance. An endowment to provide salaries for a body of judges, needful in itself, was suggested to the Pope as a proper purpose for imposing upon the Scottish prelacies the permanent tax of £10,000 a year.

The idea that the members of the Court of Session should constitute a "College of Justice" probably originated with Sir Thomas Erskine, who, according to the Imperial Ambassador in Rome, had been a student at the University of Pavia, where, as in other Italian cities, there was a *Collegium Dominorum Judicum*. In Pavia "at the beginning of the sixteenth century the college was in a most flourishing condition, and enjoyed special privileges imperial and papal."[5] Therefore to request money for the endowment of a College of Justice was acceptable to the Pope as a request to endow an institution thoroughly approved of and understood in Italy. As a guarantee that the Pope's generosity would have results beneficial to the church it was arranged that in the membership of the College of Justice ecclesiastics would predominate: of the fifteen "senators" to be appointed seven were to be spiritual and seven temporal persons, and the president was always to be an ecclesiastic. On 13th September 1531 the institution of the College of Justice was announced in a papal bull which declared that the Scottish prelacies were to provide £10,000 annually for its endowment as long as James V and his successors remained faithful to Rome.

At the beginning of its existence the College of Justice was more a matter of nomenclature than a new institution. Of the fifteen senators appointed in 1532 fourteen, including the president, Alexander Mylne, Abbot of Cambuskenneth, had served on the Session in 1531; while eleven of them had served on it since 1527. Furthermore, it was decided in 1532 that although the college had a permanent president in the person of the Abbot of Cambuskenneth, "the Chancellor, if he chose to attend, was to occupy the chair; and a limited number of additional lords were introduced . . ."[6] This was not very different from Archbishop Dunbar's arrangement of 1531. It was no wonder that to James V's contemporaries the College of Justice did not appear to be the great innovation which many historians present it as having been. At the time what seemed the most important aspect of it was its endowment.

Inevitably the "Great Tax" was unpopular with the Scottish prelates, not only because of the financial burden which it imposed on them, but also because they had no illusions about its purpose. James V was not totally cynical in his dealings with the College of Justice, for he had every intention of paying the senators their salaries; but as the prelates realized, the salaries would be a small proportion of the "Great Tax", and the rest would go to recoup the finances of the Crown. The leader of those prelates who were disposed to resist was Archbishop Beaton, never in favour with the King, jealous of the preferment of Archbishop Dunbar to the chancellorship, and a creditor of the Crown to the extent of £860, which he had been forced to lend in 1525. Even Dunbar himself, who was greatly concerned with the efficient administration of justice, and was one of the three executors of the papal bull, was not enthusiastic over the extent of the taxation. He fell into arrears with his own payments. James dealt with Beaton by putting him on trial for treasonable intercourse with England, and keeping him for a time under house arrest; with the rest of his prelates he dealt in a more compromising spirit. He agreed that instead of paying him £10,000 a year in perpetuity they should compound for the sum of £72,000 to be paid in four instalments. The salaries of the senators of the College of Justice were to be paid out of a tax of £1,400 *per annum*, to be paid from the incomes of benefices assigned for the purpose, with the addition of £200 *per annum* from benefices in the patronage of the Crown, a somewhat meagre provision. This arrangement was ratified by a bull of Pope Paul III in March 1535.

*　　*　　*

To revert to the events of 1531, the imposition of the "Three Teinds" and the "Great Tax" promised the King a speedy alleviation of his financial difficulties. The financial possibilities of marriage remained yet to be exploited.

Upon Pope Clement VII's refusal of the hand of Catherine de Medici James reverted to his persistent desire to induce François Ier to honour the Treaty of Rouen. The Imperial proposals still had their uses as the means to put pressure on the French King. Charles V continued to court the Scottish Alliance, and not with proposals of marriage only; in 1532 he sent James V the Order of the Golden Fleece, an honour which no previous King of Scots had received. It was probably the fear of losing Scotland to the Imperial alliance which caused François Ier to adopt a more positive policy. He had pleaded repeatedly, and with truth, that Madeleine was too young for marriage; now it seemed that she was too delicate. Indeed, it was feared that she would follow her sisters Louise and Charlotte to an early death.

In the summer of 1533 François suggested that in place of Madeleine James should have his choice of three ladies of the highest nobility of France: Marie de Bourbon, daughter of the Duc de Vendôme; Marie de Guise, daughter of the Duc de Guise; or Isabeau d'Albret, daughter of François' brother-in-law, the King of the little state of Navarre. James was not flattered by this suggestion, for the Treaty of Rouen had promised him a Daughter of France; but he played with the suggestion, as he continued to play with the Imperial proposals. To outbid François the Emperor offered James the choice of three Maries of Imperial blood; Mary of Portugal, Mary of Hungary, or Mary of England. This offer was more magniloquent than realistic, for only Mary of Portugal was in fact available. Mary of Hungary absolutely declined to marry the King of Scots, for he was years younger than herself and his realm was a distant *terra incognita*. As far as Mary of England was concerned, the Emperor had not the power to bestow her in marriage. However, the offer of the English princess shortly came from the King who had that power, her father.

In the year 1534 the Treaty of Berwick, made between Scotland and England in 1529, was due to expire. As the time of its expiry approached disturbances on the Borders increased until there was a condition of undeclared war. Both Kings were eager to renew the treaty; James, whose attitude to England was entirely unmilitaristic, because he wished to keep his Kingdom in peace, the Border included; Henry, because his energies were occupied by the religious and political situation in England. Henry, indeed, proposed to deal with his nephew as his father had dealt with James IV: to tie Scotland to England by a marriage alliance while he dealt with the difficult affairs of his own realm. Then, if he should become embroiled with either France or the Empire, the marriage should serve to prevent Scotland from allying with either of them.

The King of Scots was not to be caught in this fashion.

His father's experience of an English marriage alliance did not encourage repetition. Furthermore, the status of the Princess Mary had been reduced by the marriage of Henry VIII and Anne Boleyn, and by the birth in September 1533 of the Princess Elizabeth. Mary was no longer Princess of Wales; upon the birth of her half-sister she had been declared a bastard. Even had he wished to make an English marriage, James V could scarcely have regarded her as a worthy match. However, on 12th May 1534 peace between England and Scotland, a matter of expediency to both Kings, was signed; the peace was to last for the joint lifetime of both, and for one year beyond the death of whichever should die first. James, having achieved advantageous peace terms and declined the hand of Mary, made Henry VIII a gracious and soothing concession; he recognized the validity of the English King's divorce from Catherine of Aragon and of his marriage to Anne Boleyn. Henry set a high value upon such a concession from a Catholic sovereign, and he decided, as a mark of his appreciation, to bestow on his nephew the Order of the Garter. It was delivered to James on 4th May 1535 by Lord William Howard, younger brother of the Duke of Norfolk.*

It may well have been this concession on the part of James that led Henry to consider the possibility of persuading his nephew to follow his example in breaking with the Papacy and claiming supremacy over the church within his kingdom. To examine the possibility, Henry sent William Barlow, Bishop-elect of St Asaph, to Scotland in the autumn of 1535. Barlow's observations were not encouraging. He reported that James was under the influence of ecclesiastical counsellors who were all "the Pope's pestilential creatures, and very limbs of the Devil."[7] Nevertheless, Henry was not deterred. In January 1536 Lord William Howard and Barlow were despatched together on an embassy to

* Norfolk, who succeeded to his dukedom in 1524, has been mentioned previously as Earl of Surrey, on p. 46.

Scotland. Howard was instructed to explain to James the nature of Henry VIII's ecclesiastical policy, to "inculce and harpe uppon the spring of honour and proffit", and to propose to James a meeting between himself and Henry, which should take place at York. Barlow was to present the King of Scots with his book "The Doctrine of a Christian Man", of which Henry thought very highly, and also to besiege him with persuasive oratory. James expressed willingness to meet his uncle, but refused to go any further into England than Newcastle-upon-Tyne; Henry inevitably refused to go any further north than York, and so the projected meeting was deferred indefinitely. In any case, Henry's wish to discuss with his nephew the application to Scotland of an ecclesiastical policy similar to his own was shown to be futile by James's uncompromising reception of Barlow. He refused even to accept "The Doctrine of a Christian Man". Barlow nonetheless persisted in making an oration denouncing the Papacy, but he was interrupted by the onset of a thunderstorm. James completed Barlow's confusion by crossing himself and exclaiming that he did not know which he feared more, the thunder of heaven or the thunder of Barlow's blasphemy.[8]

James had already shown himself and his kingdom committed to Rome by his dealings both with the papacy and with such manifestations of the Reformation as had appeared in Scotland. In an act of Parliament of 1532 the King's resolution was recorded to "defend the authority, liberty and freedom of the seat of Rome and halikirk."[9] (i.e. the Holy Church) This was, of course, an official assurance that the Pope's generosity over the "Three Teinds" and the "Great Tax" would be properly earned; but the government of Scotland, both during the minority of James V and since the beginning of his personal rule, had dealt with the onset of the Reformation in an entirely orthodox fashion.

The active beginning of the Reformation in Europe is often conveniently if arbitrarily dated from Luther's sym-

bolic gesture of defiance in nailing his ninety-five theses to
the church door in Wittenberg in 1517. The Reformation
was slow in coming to Scotland. It was recognised by the
government as a threat to the orthodoxy of the country in
1525, when the importation of Lutheran books was banned
by act of Parliament. But Lutheran books and copies of
Tyndale's English translation of the New Testament
continued to be shipped to the east coast ports "the most
part to the town of St Andrews." As the seat of an archbishopric and the university, and as a gateway to the con-
tinent, St Andrews was a city of importance and intellectual
activity, and it was at the centre of the scene in all phases
of the Reformation conflict. At St Andrews occurred the
first Protestant martyrdom: that of Patrick Hamilton,
commendator or titular Abbot of Ferne, in 1528. Every
aspect of this martyrdom served to make it sensational.
Hamilton was of high birth and was related by marriage to
Archbishop Beaton. This could not save him from condemnation, but it was an embarrassment to Beaton, for
Hamilton, with the provocative moral courage which is so
often an ingredient in the character of a martyr, had taken
a post in the University of St Andrews. He was the author
of a widely read religious treatise; he was also an attractive
personality and an extremely brave man. His execution by
burning aroused a great deal of public compassion, since
it took place upon a day of rain, when the fire would not burn
vigorously enough to give him a quick death. The exem-
plary courage with which he bore a six hour martyrdom could
only serve to advertise his Lutheran ideas and to show up
orthodox Catholicism in its most unattractive guise. The
dangerous power of Patrick Hamilton's example was
recognised by one of Beaton's servants, who said to the
Archbishop that if he proposed to burn more heretics,
then "let them be burnt in deep cellars, for the reek of
Master Patrick Hamilton has infected as many as it blew
upon." Beaton, however, remained convinced of the

François I attributed to Joos van Cleef

James V by an unknown artist

efficacy of execution as a deterrent to the spread of heresy. In 1532 or 1533 he condemned as a heretic a man named Henry Forrest, who was burnt on the highest point of the cliffs at St Andrews.

James V himself, though solidly orthodox, was not an immoderate persecutor. He was probably influenced by the moderation of Archbishop Dunbar, who was opposed to Beaton in this matter as in all others. In 1534 James presided "all cled in red"[10] (red was the judicial costume of the time) at the trial for heresy of David Straiton, brother of the Laird of Laurieston, and Norman Gourlay, a priest. Straiton, who had quarrelled with the Bishop of Moray on the subject of tithes, derived some of his income from fishing; and, following the quarrel, he commanded his servants to throw every tenth fish of their catch back into the sea. The tithe-collectors, he suggested, should seek the dues they claimed where he had caught the fish. James was well aware of the shortcomings of the clergy, amongst which a taste for good living and worldly goods was one much criticized. Probably he felt that Straiton was being accused of heresy when his fault was anticlericalism. He was disposed to acquit Straiton, but the clergy on the tribunal told him that in cases involving heresy he did not possess the prerogative of mercy. James submitted to their judgment, and both Straiton and Gourlay were burnt on 27th August 1534. However, "Compared with other countries, the Reformation in Scotland . . . made few martyrs. In all, seven Protestants suffered death by law before the Reformation and two Catholics after it."[11] Even the zeal of Archbishop Beaton and later that of his nephew David, Cardinal Beaton, was not manifested numerically. As far as James himself was concerned, he gave the Pope a sufficient display of orthodoxy by the assurance offered in his act of Parliament, by his resistance to the persuasions of Henry VIII, and by the small scale persecution which he countenanced. He managed also to convince his uncle, for the time being, that he had no intention of leading Scotland the way that England had gone.

While handling his diplomatic relations with England with skill and firmness, James continued his efforts to achieve an advantageous French marriage. His choice of the auld alliance was not prompted merely by the blind traditionalism of which some historians have accused him. He was wise enough to see the advisability of maintaining peace with England; at the same time he was not unwise in suspecting Henry VIII's motives in offering a marriage alliance. France might prove herself an ungenerous ally, but at least geographical considerations made it less likely that she would swallow Scotland whole.

At the end of 1534 François Ier, genuinely unwilling to part with Madeleine, made James a definite offer of Marie de Bourbon, daughter of the Duc de Vendôme, with a dowry of 100,000 crowns. The King of Scots received a flattering portrait of Marie to encourage him to accept; but it was reported to him that both she and her younger sister were "sore made awrye". James's desire for an alliance with France proved stronger than his disappointment over the Princess Madeleine. He decided to marry Marie de Bourbon, but in addition to her dowry he demanded an annuity of 20,000 *livres* and the Order of St Michael. In July 1535 he appointed a commission, which included the Duke of Albany, to negotiate the terms of the marriage; but his attitude was transparently unenthusiastic, and his official letter to the Duc de Vendôme would have left the latter in no doubt that his daughter was considered very much inferior to the Daughter of France.[12] Nevertheless, the marriage contract was successfully negotiated, perhaps with little active participation by Albany, for he died before the contract was confirmed by François Ier on 29th March 1536. In April François duly sent James the St Michael, which was delivered to him by his half-brother Moray. James was highly gratified by his possession of the three leading European orders of chivalry. He later had the insignia of the Orders of the Golden Fleece, the Garter and the St Michael carved above the Outer Entry of the Palace of Linlithgow.

James's lack of enthusiasm for the Vendôme marriage was accompanied and perhaps increased by a resurgence of his love for Margaret Erskine. Suddenly the considerations of the dowry and the auld alliance decreased in importance; in his disinclination to marry Marie the King had a more than passing desire to let go everything for which he had worked so patiently, and marry his mistress. In 1533 she had borne him a son who was given the royal name of James Stewart. Years later, when in favour with his half-sister Mary, Queen of Scots, he was granted the title of Earl of Moray, and subsequently he became Regent of Scotland during the minority of Mary's son James VI. He was a most astute politician, and probably totally unscrupulous, but he went down to history as "the Good Regent". Perhaps it is a matter for regret that James V did not marry Margaret Erskine, for almost certainly their son would have proved an extremely able King. However, by 1536 Margaret was married to Sir William Douglas of Lochleven. James, determined to marry her, arranged a divorce in Scotland and wrote to Pope Paul III requesting a dispensation for the marriage. In May it was reported that James would "not be dissuaded from marrying the divorced gentlewoman";[13] and by June the Emperor was informed that James had actually married "une sienne amoureuse."[14] But on 30th June the Pope sent James his refusal to recognize the validity of the Scottish divorce. Margaret therefore could not lawfully remarry; apparently she returned to her husband, for she remained 'the Lady of Lochleven' for the rest of her life. When Mary, Queen of Scots was imprisoned in Lochleven Castle in 1567, the Lady of Lochleven, embittered by the unkindness of fate which had brought her so near to being Queen herself, neglected no opportunity to slight and insult the unfortunate Mary, who she said was herself a bastard, while her own son the Earl of Moray was the legitimate child of James V and therefore the rightful King. Perhaps the Lady of Lochleven had convinced herself of this in the course of many years' brooding over her misfortune; or perhaps she and the King had even gone through some form of marriage in anticipation of the Pope's consent. His refusal was inevitably a greater disaster to her than to the King.

James accepted his disappointment in a more obedient spirit than Henry VIII had done in similar circumstances. Political and financial considerations reasserted themselves in his mind, and he prepared to go through with the Vendôme marriage.

In July 1536 James decided to pay an unofficial visit to France to see his prospective bride. He sailed from Leith with a small entourage all contained aboard one ship. The sea was extremely rough, and the pilot asked the King, if it should be necessary to make for harbour, "to what coast he should direct his course"? James replied "To any thou best likest, except towards England".

He then retired to his cabin, where he managed to get some sleep in spite of the storm. While he was asleep the weather worsened, and "these who accompanied him command(ed) the pilot to turn his sails again for Scotland . . . so when the King awoke he found himself near his own harbours upon the Forth"[15] Furiously angry, he blamed Sir James Hamilton of Finnart, who was the most important person in his entourage, for making the decision. Indeed, with his ready suspicion of the greater nobility, he immediately assumed that the Hamiltons were opposed to his marriage as a threat to their proximity to the succession, and that Finnart his favourite had been acting as the tool of family ambition. Finnart fell into considerable disfavour for the supposed motive of his supposed decision, without being allowed the slightest chance to justify himself.

James took the opportunity provided by his unintended return to prepare a more lavish expedition, and, while it was in preparation he made a pilgrimage on foot to the shrine of Our Lady of Loretto near Musselburgh, a few miles outside Edinburgh. This shrine had been founded about three years previously by a hermit named Thomas Duthie whose career had included captivity among the Turks and life as a hermit on Mount Sinai. He brought from Loretto in Italy the image of Our Lady for which he built the shrine.

Since the hermit of Loretto was represented by both Knox[16] and Buchanan as a gross imposter, the assumption inevitably arose that James V was readily taken in by religious imposture. James, however, whose religion seems to have been typically that of a non-intellectual orthodox Catholic of the period, did not, of course, share the reformers' view that the spiritual claims of the church were invalidated by the human failings of its servants. He did not make his pilgrimage to show his approbation of Thomas Duthie, but to venerate Our Lady of Loretto. Whatever failings Duthie may or may not have had the distinction would have remained clear to the King.[17]

In his private life James exhibited a by no means uncommon blend of piety and immorality; in his public life he showed himself an obedient son of the church, which did not restrain him from driving hard bargains with the Holy Father. He would not follow the example of Henry VIII, but the Pope must reward him accordingly. There was not only the business of the College of Justice, there was also the matter of the King's bastard sons, for whom he induced the Pope to make generous provision in similar fashion, from Scottish benefices. In February 1533 James had written to Pope Clement VII admitting that he was the father of three illegitimate sons and requesting that notwithstanding their defect of birth, they should be permitted to hold benefices in plurality; and further, that on reaching

their twentieth year they should become eligible for prima-
tial, archiepiscopal and episcopal preferment.[18] Clement VII
acquiesced in this request, and Paul III, though adamant
over Margaret Erskine's divorce, was obliging in the matter
of making provision for the King's later children. James
Stewart, the King's eldest son by Elizabeth Shaw, became
Commendator or titular Abbot of Kelso and Melrose;
James Stewart *Secundus*, his son by Margaret Erskine,
became Prior of St Andrews; Robert Stewart, his son by
Euphemia Elphinstone, became Prior of Holyrood; John
Stewart, his son by Elizabeth Carmichael, became Prior
of Coldingham; and Adam Stewart, his son by Elizabeth
Stewart, became Prior of the Charterhouse of Perth. However, the King had long ago written to Albany that he wished
to marry partly "pour evyter la procréation des batardz";
by 1536 he was eager to bring protracted marriage diplomacy to a conclusion.

On 1st September James set sail for France for the
second time. On this occasion his entourage filled seven
ships. It included the Earls of Moray, Argyll and Rothes,
and the young Earl of Arran — the son of that Earl who
had played a prominent part in the political life of Scotland
during the King's minority, and who had died in 1530.
In character the younger Arran very much resembled his
father, for he also was intelligent but suggestible, and was
similarly cursed with a shifting instability of mind. The
King was accompanied also by the Lords Maxwell, Fleming
and Erskine, and by Oliver Sinclair, "a cadet of the almost
princely house of Caithness and Roslin",[19] who gradually
came to replace Sir James Hamilton of Finnart in his affections and became that magnet of unpopularity, the King's
"minion". The royal expedition, which sailed from Kirkcaldy, reached Dieppe on 10th September. The King
immediately set out for St Quentin, where the Duc de
Vendôme held his court.

Lindsay of Pitscottie tells how the King, in order to see Marie de Bourbon while remaining unrecognized, disguised himself as the servant of one of his own servants. But Marie, who had in her possession a portrait of the King of Scots "passed to her coffer and took out his picture . . . and as soon as she looked at the said picture she knew the King incontinent (i.e. immediately) where he stood among the rest of his company." She at once went up to him "and took him by the hand and said 'Sir, you stand o'er far aside' ", and greeted him as "your grace". Then "the King hearing this was a little ashamed that he had disguised himself to be unknown and then was so hastily known by the means of that gentlewoman." He was obliged to acknowledge his identity and permit himself to be presented to the Duc de Vendôme, who entertained him with the greatest magnificence:

"There was made by the Duke of Wandoun (sic) a fair palace royal with all costly ornaments and apparel to do the King honour; to wit – the walls thereof hung with fine tapestry of cloth of gold and fine silk, the floor laid over with fine silk, the bed hung with French cloth of gold, and also a pall of gold set with precious stones set above the King when he sat at meat, and the halls and chambers was all perfumed with sweet odours which was very costly and delectable to the sense of men. There was nothing left by the Duke of Wandoun that might be done to the King of Scotland's honour."

James remained at St Quentin eight days. In public he treated Marie de Bourbon with the utmost courtesy, but he was disappointed with her appearance; in private he admitted that she was "bossue et contre-faicte", or, as she had been described to him, "sore made awrye." Some time during the eight days which he spent face to face with disappointment, James apparently decided to cut the diplomatic knot by demanding Madeleine under circumstances which would make it almost impossible for François Ier to refuse her. If he actually resolved to call François' bluff in this way he succeeded superbly.

* * *

In the year of James V's visit the King of France was forty-two. He was dark haired and dark skinned, and in his youth had been considered extremely handsome. A superb physique, spontaneous charm and *élan de vie* combined to make him a brilliantly attractive personality. But middle age, which had brought him ill health and many griefs, had somewhat dimmed the splendour and brilliance of his image. Self indulgence and "galanteries excessives" had given his swarthy face, with its prominent drooping nose and heavy lidded eyes, an expression unpleasingly reminiscent of a satyr.

By his first wife, Claude de France, the daughter of his predecessor Louis XII, the King had had three sons, François, Henri and Charles, and four daughters. Of the daughters, Louise and Charlotte were already dead. Their mother was dead also, and the surviving daughters, Madeleine and Marguerite had been brought up by their Aunt, Marguerite Queen of Navarre, François' remarkable sister, the author of the *Heptameron*, the patroness of Clement Marot, and the protectress of the French Reformers. The royal children had acquired a stepmother in 1530, the Emperor's sister Eleanor of Portugal, forced upon François as the pledge of a disadvantageous peace, when the fortunes of the Emperor were in the ascendant. That Eleanor of Portugal was unloved was the almost inevitable consequence of such a bargain. She was not permitted to have the care of the King's children, neither did she bear him any children herself. The uneasy peace which followed this unhappy political marriage lasted six years, and was broken in 1536 by an imperial invasion of Provence, provoked by François' anti-imperialist diplomacy. When James V landed in France the rumour had spread before him that he had come to bring military aid to the King of France. But in fact by the time of James's arrival the Emperor had been defeated already. He had found Provence devastated before his line of advance, and had been forced to withdraw from a desert in which his army could not maintain itself.

James, however, did not find a court rejoicing over the Emperor's defeat, but a court in mourning for the death of the King's eldest son, the Dauphin François, who had died at Lyons in August, suddenly and mysteriously. It was generally believed that he had been poisoned, and his Italian Squire Montecuculli, who had brought him a drink immediately before he fell ill, died an appalling death for the supposed crime, of which he had first admitted and then denied knowledge, under torture. If the Dauphin was indeed poisoned, the author of the crime was never discovered. For the King it was an additional sorrow that he had lost an heir of whom he had had great hopes, and whom he had greatly loved, whose place had been taken by the sombre and reserved Henri, Duc d'Orléans, the husband of Catherine de Medici, a son with whom François had little in common. The King was prostrated by his grief. He fell ill with it, and the Court remained at Lyons.

When the King of Scots arrived at Lyons he was received by the new Dauphin Henri, who with an exceptional display of enthusiasm, "ran to him and gat him in his arms and welcomed him very favourably, and showed him that his father would be marvellously blythe and rejoiced of his coming, considering how it stood with him at that time." He told James of the poisoning of the Dauphin François, and of the grief and illness of the King. He then brought James to the King's bedchamber, and knocked loudly and unceremoniously on the door. From within François demanded who had come to disturb him, to which Henri answered "It is the King of Scotland come to see your Grace and to give you comfort."

On hearing these words François, with characteristic

resilience, "bounded from his bed and opened the chamber door and received the King of Scotland in his arms, thanking God of (i.e. for) His great benefits." It had pleased God, he went on, to take away one of his sons, but it had also pleased Him to send "that noble Prince" the King of Scots to take his place.

To this James responded in kind by requesting the King of France not to treat him with the formality due to a visiting sovereign, but with the informal affection proper to a son. François thereupon requested Henri to entertain the King of Scots as if he were his own brother, and he himself showed him "love and favour so fervently as he had been his own natural son gotten of his body."[20] Later, when James made his state entry into Paris, François commanded the deputation from the *Parlement de Paris* which received him to wear scarlet gowns, as they would for the reception of the Dauphin. The Parlement protested that its members were accustomed to receive foreign royalties clad in black; but François overrode the protest and James was received as a son of France, by a deputation in scarlet.

At Lyons James first met the Princess who, throughout the complexities of his marriage diplomacy, had always been his first choice. The Princess Madeleine is always described as a frail and exquisite beauty, but the only likeness of her which the author has seen, an illumination in the late sixteenth century Seton Armorial fails to capture an impression either of frailness or of beauty. It shows her as an almost stalwart little figure in a heraldic dress which has a blue skirt embroidered with silver fleurs-de-lys, a rose-coloured bodice and overskirt, and silver sleeves. The heraldry being more important in an armorial than the portraiture, this picture may not resemble the real Madeleine very closely. But since a likeness has definitely been attempted and achieved in depicting James V, who stands at her side holding the lion banner of the King of Scots, perhaps as an indication of Madeleine's appearance the picture should not be dismissed. It shows her as pale skinned and fair haired, unlike most of the Valois family, but with the same heavy lidded eyes and prominent drooping nose as her father, François. If her beauty was not in her features, then perhaps the impression of beauty was conveyed by her delicate colouring and the splendour and elegance of her dress, by the grace of her bearing and by her charm, which all acknowledged.

According to Pitscottie when James first saw the Princess Madeleine she was "riding in a chariot, because she was sickly . . . she might not ride on horse. Yet notwithstanding all her sickness and malady, from (the) time she saw the King of Scotland she became so enamoured with him that she would have no man living but him only . . ."

The marriage of James and Madeleine is generally represented as the romantic conclusion of the protracted negotiations for the King's marriage. James had played the part of the knight errant and Madeleine that of the *princesse lointaine* to perfection; that they should fall in love seemed the natural consequence. Yet Pitscottie does not suggest that James fell in love with the French princess. His version is that the enamoured Madeleine was determined to marry the King of Scots, and that he "consented thereto hastily for the love that he bore to the King of France. And also he knew there was great profit, friendship and alliance to be gotten at the King of France's hand."[21] In other words he was more concerned with the auld alliance than with the Princess herself. The Abbé de Brantôme, who equals Pitscottie as a purveyor of vivid and romantic versions of any incident, presents an unromantic view of the marriage from the other side. According to Brantôme Madeleine's desire was not to marry the man with whom she had fallen in love at first sight, but to be a queen, "so proud and lofty was her heart." Her father continued to doubt the wisdom of allowing the marriage, upon which the two principals were so determined, for he feared that it would hasten the Princess's expected death. But Madeleine's reply to words of caution was "At least I shall be queen for so long as I live; that is what I have always wished for"[22] – a reply redolent not of romantic love but of renaissance *magnanimity*, well enough defined by Brantôme's reference to her proud and lofty heart. Both the King of Scots and the French princess had grown up with the expectation that they would marry each other in accordance with the Treaty of Rouen; but the political situation of Europe had kept François so long unwilling to honour the treaty that to both the King and the Princess the marriage had become a matter more of ambition than of expectation. James's success in finally bringing François to consent was a triumph both diplomatic and personal.

The conventions of court poetry, both French and Scots, demanded that the union of James and Madeleine should be represented as a triumph of love. In the poetry which celebrated the occasion lay the origin of the romantic myth. To Sir David Lindsay, James V is Madeleine's "prince and paramour", and in an anonymous *Elegie Nuptiale* addressed to Madeleine the red-haired King of Scots becomes *Ton blond Phébus, ton mignon coinct et doulx* and the poet bids the royal lovers, whom he addresses as doves

> . . . bec a bec succez l'ame profonde
> De l'ung et l'autre, embrassez, acollez,
> Jouez, riez, l'ung a l'aultrez vollez . . .
> Trois cens Venus adorez dans ung jour
> Au grand Hymen entendez sans sejour . . .[23]

This was the conventional metamorphosis of a political marriage!

The marriage contract was signed at Blois on 26th November, and the marriage took place on 1st January 1537 in the Cathedral of Notre Dame in Paris. It was graced with the presence of three kings – the bridegroom himself, the King of France and the King of Navarre – and

seven cardinals. James came to the altar dressed in white and
gold, his face marked by a bruise he had got in one of the
tournaments which celebrated the occasion. There was a
certain piquancy in the fact that the ceremony itself was
performed by the Cardinal de Bourbon, the Duc de Vendôme's brother. What became of the disappointed Marie
herself was various reported. It was said that she disdain-
fully refused a lesser match with a French nobleman, and
that she "turned religious" (i.e. became anun). Pitscottie's
more dramatic story was that she "took such displeasure
at the King of Scotland's marriage with Madeleine that
she deceased immediately thereafter, whereat the King of
Scotland was heavily displeased, thinking he was the occasion of that gentlewoman's death." If that were true it
suggests that even though he was self absorbed at least
he was not wholly devoid of self-criticism.

The marriage of James and Madeleine was celebrated
with such splendour that "there was never so great solemnity
and triumph seen in France in one day since the time of
King Charles the Maine (i.e. Charlemagne). For there was
such jousting and tournaments both on horse and on foot
and in burgh and land (i.e. town and country) and also
upon the sea in ships, and so mickle artillery set (i.e. fired
off) in all parts of France both on the land and on the sea
and also in castles and towns and villages that no man might
hear for the reird (i.e. roar) of them."[24] François who had
an insatiable delight in pageants and lavish entertainments
and took advantage of every possible occasion which
provided an excuse to organize them, seems to have sur-
passed himself in providing sumptuous displays to celebrate
the marriage of his daughter. Pitscottie thought that only
"igramansie" (i.e. necromancy) could account for such
wonders as "flying dragons in the air" which spurted fire
from their heads and tails, or "great rivers of water running
through the town and ships fighting thereupon . . . with
shooting of guns like cracks of thunder." The staging of

mock sea-fights was the latest fashion in public spectacle, and had not yet been seen in Scotland, which explains Pitscottie's naive wonder; but this is not to say that Scotland was incapable of producing entertainments of elegance and splendour, as had been shown by the Earl of Atholl's entertainment of James V in 1530, which had impressed even a visitor from Italy.

By the time the marriage took place James had been four months in France, but still he showed no haste to return to Scotland. No doubt the danger of a winter voyage to Madeleine's frail health provided a good enough pretext for deferring their departure until the spring. James learnt a great deal from his sojourn in France, and later attempted to apply some of the lessons he had learnt to his own kingdom. He greatly admired the splendour, the comfort and the elaborately organized ritual with which the King of France surrounded himself in his royal châteaux at Blois, at Chambord or at Fontainebleau. James's stay in France gave him an opportunity to admire at leisure the architectural magnificence of François' building works, the beauty of the decorative schemes which embellished their interiors and the excellence of the sculpture, pictures and *objets de vertu* which they contained. François, a wholehearted admirer of Italian renaissance style in all aspects of the arts, could command, and afford to employ, an array of genius which encompassed Leonardo da Vinci at the beginning of the reign and Benvenuto Cellini at the end of it. His court, which rivalled the papacy in artistic patronage, could not itself be rivalled by the distant and relatively poor Court of Scotland. But evidently James decided that what he could not rival he could at least reproduce to whatever extent his resources would permit. After his return to Scotland the enlargement and improvement of his own palaces, the enrichment of their interiors, and the increased size of the royal household, all mirrored his appreciation of the Court of France, and his recognition of the fact that patronage of the arts, beyond being a civilized pleasure, directly served to enhance the prestige of the sovereign.

In this particular matter also James doubtless would have wished to imitate François Ier, who throughout his reign worked to enhance his own power and prestige by reducing the feudal nobility to a class of courtiers dependent upon the favour of the King. To a certain extent he succeeded. At least he succeeded in imposing upon his nobility the necessity of frequent residence at Court: "Pour soliciter directement le monarque, obtenir une faveur, le renouvellement d'un privilège, il est necessaire de paraitre."[25] And to appear continually in the presence of the King necessitated an expensive and exhausting existence in which the nobility trailed around France in the wake of a King who was perpetually on progress. In order to remain in his company, in the words of Marot "les plus grands logeront en greniers." The extent of François' success must have seemed admirable to James V, whose own powerful subjects habitually expressed disaffection with the royal policy by absenting themselves from Court; and, once absent, their actions were of course beyond the King's control. James could deal with disaffected lords individually, he could imprison one and banish another; a disaffected class was a danger which he could not afford, and one which had shown itself increasingly throughout the years of his personal rule. To work for the general support of the nobility, as James IV had done, would have been his wisest course; only then would the next step of making the nobility dependent upon the King have become feasible. It remained beyond the scope of James V.

However, while he remained in France, entertained with a continual round of tournaments, pageants and elaborate civic receptions, the problems of Scotland were perhaps as remote from James's mind as they ever could be. France offered some minor problems of its own: for instance, a linguistic problem, for although James could write French adequately he could not speak it fluently. The English Ambassadors in France, Stephen Gardiner, Bishop of Winchester and Sir John Wallop, with whom James showed some reluctance to communicate, wrote rather amusingly of his inability to converse with the French:

"He is a man of the fewest words that may be. The ambassador of Venice was with him, and spake a long matter unto him, and neither by himself ne (nor) any other answered him one word. He spake not unto us very many. His wife should temper him well, for she can speak; and if she spake as little as he, the house should be very quiet."[26]

Pierre Liset, *Premier Président* of the *Parlement de Paris*, had much the same story to tell when he recorded James's reception by the Parlement upon his state entry into Paris on the last day of December 1536, the day before his marriage. James, dressed in a coat of "cramasy velvet, encrusted and fringed with gold, fastened with horns and lined with red taffeta", was received by the scarlet-clad deputation from the Parlement. Liset wrote "After reverence had been shown to the said King of Scots, Monsieur *le Premier Président* made him an oration on behalf of the said court of the Parlement; the which being done, the said King of Scots embraced the said Présidents, without saying a single word to them, since he has little knowledge of the French tongue."[27]

But in spite of this difficulty James obviously enjoyed himself immensely in France; and, as usual not content only with the formal entertainments provided for him, he took the opportunity to mingle with the people. An agent of the Douglases, one John Penven, wrote for their amusement a mocking account of the King of Scots going shopping in Paris, and "with a servant or two running up and down the streets of Paris buying every trifle himself, and every carter pointing at him and paying 'Yonder goes la roy de Escosse' (sic)."[28] The "trifles" included white plumes to

The Palace Block, Stirling Castle

The Courtyard Façade, south range, Falkland Palace

'Stirling Head' traditionally identified as James V

deck his own bonnet and the headpiece of his horse in a
tournament, and a great pointed diamond which cost him
8,787 francs 10 shillings Scots!

Penven evidently had access to good sources of information in the King's household; his reports of political events
are accurate and his gossip is illuminating. He reported to
Sir George Douglas that James had sent letters and tokens
to the Lady of Lochleven, and that Hamilton of Finnart
was still out of favour. Apparently during the voyage to
France James had said to one of his attendants "If I would
but once look merely upon the Earl of Angus, Sir James
would droop; for by the wounds of God, for all Sir James's
bragging, the Earl of Angus and he never met but Sir
James turned ever the back seams of his hose." This remark
made Douglas sympathizers imagine that Angus had a
chance of regaining the King's favour, and Penven's letters
are full of encouragement: "You have no foe with the King
save the Earl of Argyll", and "The Earl (of Moray) whis-
pered to a friend of yours 'where is your masters now? . . .
They should have now friends enough.' "[29] Penven therefore
suggested that Henry VIII should be induced to write to
François Ier in Angus's favour, and Madeleine be persuaded
to plead for him to the King of Scots. But all this hopeful
scheming came to nothing. James had no intention of looking
upon the Earl of Angus, and perhaps had only mentioned
the possibility by way of baiting and worrying Finnart. It
was also reported to the Douglases that at some time while
James was in France the Earl of Moray asked him "where
his minion Sir James Hamilton was"? He replied that his
minion had "fawtted so sore to him" (i.e. had offended
him so much) that he would never show favour to him
again. Apparently Finnart had been in such high favour
with the King that Moray found James's reply frankly
incredible. His coarse retort was "He could not fawt to
you if he dryte (i.e. shit) in your hands." However the King
had meant what he said. Finnart never regained the degree

of favour that he had previously enjoyed, and his place in the King's affections was taken by Oliver Sinclair.

It was May by the time that James had made up his mind to leave France. Before he and his Queen set sail François Ier, who besides paying Madeleine's dowry of 100,000 *livres* had borne the whole expense of James's visit, presented him with twelve warhorses and full accoutrements for each, and with several suits of gilded armour. Madeleine was invited to select from her father's wardrobe as many lengths of cloth of gold, velvet, satin, damask and taffeta as she wished, and whatever jewels she pleased. The result was that "such substance was never seen in Scotland as this young queen brought in it." In addition François presented to James two ships named the *Salamander* and the *Morsewer*. The salamander, that mythical reptile whose natural element was fire, was the personal emblem of François Ier; the odd-sounding name 'Morsewer' was possibly either 'Monsieur', or 'Morse' (i.e. Sea-horse). The two ships served both to escort James's own fleet and to transport his enlarged entourage to Scotland. It remained to be seen whether Madeleine, whose life had been no more than a rearguard action against Death, could survive the sea voyage and endure the Scottish climate.

On 19th May, after an absence of nine months, James brought his Queen in safety to Leith. When Madeleine came ashore she knelt devoutly and "thanked God that he had safely brought her with her husband to their own country"; and, with a royal instinct for a memorable gesture, she took up two handfuls of Scottish earth and kissed it.[30] But she did not find her new country congenial, for the climate even in May was "very different from her sweet France." Nonetheless, wrote Brantôme, "without one sign of repentance, she said nothing except these words: 'Alas! I would be Queen' – covering her sadness and the fire of her ambition with the ashes of patience as best she could." Here Brantôme cannot be suspected of romancing. He describes how he came by his information: "Monsieur de Ronsard, who went with her to Scotland, told me all this; he had been a page to Monsieur d'Orléans, who allowed him to go with her, to see the world." No doubt Madeleine relied upon and confided in her French entourage, much as Mary, Queen of Scots years later relied upon those who had accompanied her from France, and turned to them for solace when Scotland proved uncongenial. Ronsard was a boy when he attended upon Madeleine; in the older Ronsard Mary also found a friend.

Madeleine might convince all but her French attendants that she was content; but she could not conceal that she was growing daily weaker. James cancelled the summer progress on which he had intended to take her, and her state entry into Edinburgh and coronation, for which Sir David Lindsay had been busily directing preparations. James decided to send her to the Abbey of Balmerino, in Fife, "as having the best airs of any places in the Kingdom"; but probably she never reached it, for on 7th July she died in Holyroodhouse.

Madeleine was greatly mourned in Scotland. The Reformers particularly lamented her, and later, during the regency of her successor, Marie de Guise, came to imagine that they had lost a potential friend of great power. Their hopes had been based on the fact that Madeleine had been brought up by François' sister, Marguerite de Navarre, so powerful a friend of the French Reformers; but whether Madeleine would have followed her example and befriended those of Scotland only time would have shown, and time was not granted her.

The most poignant lamentation for her was written by Sir David Lindsay. In his "Deploratioun of the Deith of Quene Magdalene" he describes the preparations being made for her state entry into Edinburgh, and tells how the glittering robes being made for those who would walk in her procession on the day of her coronation were all "turnit into sable" – the black gowns of mourning. The poem is addressed to Death ("thou" in the last line of the following quotation):

> Provost, bailies and lordis of the town
> The senators in order consequent
> Clad in to silk of purpure black and brown;
> Syne* the great lordis of the Parliament,
> With many knightly Baron and baurent†
> In silk and gold, in colours comfortable,
> But thou alas all turnit into sable.

As for Queen Madeleine herself:

> Under a pall of gold she should have past,
> By burgis borne, clothed in silkis fine . . .

And as she passed, "ane sight celestial", the burgesses' wives and daughters would have shouted "Vive la Royne!" At every street corner musicians would have played; "ornate orators" would have addressed to her many a "notable narration", and she would have gone at last to be crowned

> In the fair Abbey of the Holy Rude
> In presence of ane mirthful multitude.

But all this rejoicing, and all the splendour which Lindsay had been preparing for her coronation day, Death has chosen to prevent, and turned instead into "requiem aeternam" . . .[31]

Buchanan stated that public mourning was worn in Scotland for the first time for Queen Madeleine. However, this frequently repeated statement seems to be erroneous, for burgesses who were commanded to attend her funeral were bidden to bring "their blacks", which implies that they possessed mourning garments which would have been used for previous occasions.

---

* then.
† knight banneret, a knight next in rank to a baron, entitled to bring his vassals into the field under his own banner.

Though sorrow for the young Queen was great and general, the sorrow of James himself, however, was reported as being "greater nor all the laif" (i.e. than all the rest). If their marriage had not been the love match that the romantic imagination of later generations has often represented, this is not to say that there had not subsequently been love between them. Besides, James had reason to mourn her death as a threat to the alliance which he had worked so patiently to bring about; let the exigences of politics work against him, and he might well be faced with the problem of wooing the King of France to renew the auld alliance all over again. The only surviving expression of his grief for Madeleine is his official letter to François Ier, here translated:

"Monsieur,

Howbeit there could be nothing in the world more grievous than the occasion which I have for writing you this present letter – that occasion being the passing of your daughter, my most dear companion, which befell this day after long sickness – yet I would in no wise desire to be negligent in apprising you thereof. And were it not for the great comfort and confidence I have in you, that you will forever remain my good father, as I wish never to be anything but your good and humble son, I would be in greater grief than yet I am; and I assure you that you will never find any fault upon my part, who will bear myself ever towards you as a son bears himself to his father . . ."[32]

It is a letter which contains, in almost equal measures, grief for the Daughter of France and desire to retain the friendship of the King.

Chapter Six

THE ANCIENT ALLIANCE AND
THE OLD RELIGION – II

"To speak of the Emperor or the French King . . .
what can he look for at either, or at both their hands,
but fair words and entertainment for a time, as their
instrument with his own danger to serve their purposes?"

*Henry VIII. Instructions to Sir Ralph
Sadler, February* 1540.

MADELEINE's brief life was rounded by a sonorous
epitaph:

L'âme est a Dieu, le corps sommeille en transe,
Et le renom nous en demeure au monde.[1]

To be admired and dead is not perhaps wholly unenviable;
a more difficult destiny was reserved for her successor.

James's anxiety to safeguard the auld alliance was shown
by his resolution to contract a second French marriage as
quickly as possible. Indeed, his letter announcing the death
of Madeleine to François Ier announced also the impending
arrival of David Beaton, Abbot of Arbroath, on embassy.
James did not, of course, mention the purpose of this embassy in the letter; but Beaton's instructions were to negotiate the King's remarriage.

Madeleine's death, though a matter of grief to her
father, was no matter of surprise; certainly it did not cause
him to experience the slightest resentment against his son-
in-law. James's visit to France was now shown to have
been of the highest political value to him, for he had gained

the affection and respect of the King of France, who, after James's return to Scotland, showed a far greater solicitude for the auld alliance than he had shown before he made James's acquaintance. Accordingly he offered James a second French bride without hesitation, and suggested as a suitable Queen of Scotland one of the three ladies who had been on offer in 1533: Marie de Guise, who in the intervening time had been married to the Duc de Longueville and widowed in June 1537.

Since James had achieved his ambition in marrying a Daughter of France the offer of Marie de Guise no longer had the unflattering connotations that it had seemed to have in 1533. James instructed Beaton to signify to François Ier that while "Nous ne sommes point pressé de sortir de notre veuvage . . . nous voulons bien condescendre à accepter pour épouse la duchesse de Longueville."[2] James intended that Beaton should make it clear to François Ier that while he accepted Marie de Guise as a suitable bride he did not consider her the equal of his late Queen. His reported words echo the *d'haut en bas* tone in which he had signified to the Duc de Vendôme that he would condescend to accept the hand of his daughter. Beaton lost no time in relaying the message, and by 22nd October he was able to inform James that the matter was as good as settled.

Two days later, however, Jane Seymour, the third wife of Henry VIII died; and on the day following her death Henry announced to his Privy Council his intention to remarry at once. The year 1536 had been one of the most difficult years of Henry's reign. The Catholic rebellions known as the Pilgrimage of Grace had fully occupied his energies during the autumn, and he had been unable to interfere effectively to prevent the marriage of James and Madeleine and the renewal of the auld alliance. Though officially at peace with Scotland, Henry VIII was filled with suspicion and resentment against his nephew, for James had given sanctuary to many Catholic refugees from Henry's justice following the Pilgrimage of Grace, and, on his return voyage from France, while becalmed off the Yorkshire coast, he had received a deputation of Catholic gentlemen who rowed out to his ship to offer him the allegiance of the Catholics of England if he would attempt to supplant their heretic King. James, wise enough to know the limitations of his own resources, declined the offer; but Henry VIII nonetheless suspected the nature of the dealings between the King of Scots and his own disaffected subjects. The apparent insecurity of his position and his suspicions of his nephew made him more than usually desirous of weakening the position of Scotland as much as possible. The death of Jane Seymour suggested a new means of doing so.

Accordingly Henry VIII announced his intention of seeking a French marriage alliance, and declared that the fourth Queen of his choice would be Marie de Guise. The explanation of his choice was that "he was big in person and had need of a big wife": Marie de Guise was a woman of generous proportions and very tall. But undoubtedly "Henry espérait bien exciter en Ecosse un vif ressentiment contre la France et brouiller ainsi, au moins pour quelque temps, ces deux Puissances . . ."[3] The negotiations for the marriage were entrusted to Lord William Howard and the Bishop of Winchester, and Sir Peter Mewtas was sent to signify the English King's intentions to Marie de Guise herself.

The bad reputation as a husband that Henry VIII had gained by divorcing his first wife and beheading his second had been somewhat redeemed for the time being by his losing Jane Seymour through the natural misfortune of her death. It has been said often enough that Marie de Guise refused the ageing Henry VIII in favour of the young and handsome James V. In fact, she did not do so. Far from preferring James she showed a decided preference for Henry's offer, for the King of England was a greater match than the King of Scots. Nor was she necessarily only momentarily dazzled, for she was a woman whose intelligence was seldom if ever overridden by her emotions. No doubt she decided after long thought that James was not altogether the more attractive match, as opposed to the more exalted one. Admittedly the conclusions of Henry's first two marriages were far from encouraging to any prospective consort. But contrary to popular legend Henry VIII was not a great pursuer of women; indeed, his extra-marital affairs were few. His only known mistresses were Mary Boleyn, the elder sister of his second Queen, and Elizabeth Blount, the mother of his bastard, Henry Fitzroy, Duke of Richmond, who was already dead. James, on the other hand, had had the numerous mistresses previously named, and had fathered a healthy crop of bastards any of whom might possibly threaten the succession of his legitimate issue. Furthermore, at least according to the reproaches of Sir David Lindsay, he was perpetually engaged upon sexual pursuit without the slightest fastidiousness. Marie de Guise might well have argued to herself that in England the position of her children in the succession would be more secure, and that she herself would be less frequently slighted and offended. At all events, whether for personal reasons or reasons of ambition, she persuaded herself that the English match was preferable; but the fact that she was on the point of being contracted to James V placed her in a delicate position. She assured Sir Peter Mewtas that she was "preste a obéir en toutes choses au roy de France, mais qu'elle n'avait jamais consenty specialement d'estre mariée avec le roy d'Ecosse."[4]

Her words to the English envoy were in due course reported to the French ambassador in England, who in turn reported them to the King of France. François had been engaged in diplomatic exchanges with Henry VIII on the subject of the marriage, and he was furious to discover that Marie de Guise, supported by her family, was attempting independent action. At this period the Guise were "an important branch of the Valois house, not yet a separate interest in the French state, and not yet the flag-bearers of Catholicism, but a great house, still under the sway of the French King's policy."⁵ Since that policy did not include a marriage alliance with England Marie had no choice but to "obéir en toutes choses au roy de France" and reconcile herself to the prospect of marriage with James V. François firmly informed his ambassador in England "Je ne vouldroys point perdre ne alterer l'amytie d'ung ferme amy et tel que le roy d'Ecosse que j'estime comme mon propre filz." And he ordered the immediate preparation of the marriage contract. The marriage itself could be performed as soon as James had observed a decent period of mourning for Madeleine, and Marie for the Duc de Longueville.

In the brief period which intervened between his first and second marriages James dealt with a series of troubles in Scotland which were all connected in some sort with the Douglas family. He could scarcely have been unaware of the pro-Douglas feeling in his entourage while he was in France. It must, therefore, have been a considerable shock to him to discover on his return that his mother was in the midst of arranging a divorce from Lord Methven, according to whom she wished to free herself in order to remarry the Earl of Angus. But Methven, according to Margaret, had committed unforgiveable offences against her: he had appropriated rents from her dower lands, and had taken a mistress. Queen Margaret was now forty-nine, and no less masterful in temper and no less vulnerable to such injuries than she had been in her youth. Angus had long ago committed the same offences, but time perhaps had taught her to think more kindly of him; also perhaps since the auld alliance had always been against her Tudor instincts, she hoped by remarrying Angus to strengthen the English interest in Scotland. When James accused her of intending to remarry Angus Margaret fiercely denied it, and became increasingly bitter with Methven because James believed his statement in preference to her denial. To James's mind such a remarriage would have been scarcely less than treasonable. He quashed the divorce proceedings and ordered his mother to return to Lord Methven. She retired to Methven Castle as angry with her son as he was with her, and she remained married to her third husband for the few years of life that were left her.

James inevitably feared revival of sympathy for the Douglases, and feared even more the actions which might result from it. And since his undiminishing animosity against the Douglases was notorious, when two relatives of Angus went to their deaths in July 1537 it looked very much as though he were indulging in a purge of those Douglas connections remaining in Scotland.

John, Master of Forbes, was married to a sister of Angus, and had been a constant supporter of the English interest. In 1524, on the occasion of Albany's second ill-fated attempt to invade England, the Master of Forbes had been one of the instigators of the Scottish lords' mutinous refusal to follow him. In 1536 Forbes had been arrested at the instance of the Earl of Huntly, accused of the "abominable imagination" of shooting the King, *"per bumbardam sive machinam bellicam, le culvering vulgariter appellat[am]."**, when he was in Aberdeen presiding at a Justice Ayre.[6] Both the Master of Forbes and Lord Forbes his father, who was accused with him, were imprisoned while the King was in France, and on 14th July 1537 they were brought to trial. Lord Forbes was acquitted, but the Master was condemned to death and executed on the same day. It has been supposed and frequently stated, that the Master of Forbes was framed by Huntly, who also corrupted the jury, and that he had had no criminal intention whatsoever against the King.

The story of Huntly's involvement is told by Drummond

---

* by means of a bombard, or warlike machine, commonly described as a culverin.

in a curious, innuendo-laden story, which is worth quoting. According to this tale, the Master of Forbes "had for a servant or companion, and ordinary sharer of his pleasures, one named Strachan, a man come of the dreg of the people, and perfectly wicked. This man after much familiarity, and some secret service and attendance, to satisfy his insatiable desire, desired earnestly something from the Master of Forbes, which he passionately refused to give him. Upon which, carried away with rage and malice, he not only renounced his friendship and service, but betook himself to the service of his enemy the Earl of Huntly; by whose advice he forgeth a malicious plot to overthrow him. To compass their design they accuse the Master of Forbes to have had once an intention and mind to kill the King, that the Douglases might be restored to their wonted honours and ancient possessions. By price and prayers witnesses are procured to prove this against him . . ."

The record of his trial is too meagre to be of much assistance to the forming of a theory, but, according to Tytler "no previous animosity (to Forbes) can be established against Huntly, but rather the contrary; and the leniency of James, in the speedy liberation of Lord Forbes, in admitting the brother of the criminal to an office in his household, and in abstaining from the forfeiture of his estates, proved the absence of anything like vindictive feeling."[7] The guilt of the Master of Forbes was by no means universally believed in, but he was known to have been involved some years previously in a murder which had gone unpunished, and he went to his death without public sympathy. However, this was not the case with the second of Angus's relatives to be executed in the same month.

Lady Janet Douglas, a sister of Angus, was married first to Lord Glamis and then to Archibald Campbell of Skipnish, but she has gone down to history as Lady Glamis. She was accused of "treasonably conspiring and imagining the King's slaughter or destruction by poison",[8] and was tried, condemned and executed on 17th July. The sentence, which was death by burning, was carried out on the Castle Hill of Edinburgh before a large crowd. Lady Glamis was a woman of great beauty, and, said Buchanan "in her very punishment she shewed a manlike fortitude." Her death aroused great public sympathy, and the sympathizers inevitably decided that she had been innocent of conspiring the King's death, and had gone to her own for no better reason than that she was Angus's sister. Public sympathy, and quite irrationally, public belief in her innocence, increased when her husband Campbell of Skipnish, who had shared her imprisonment and witnessed her execution, fell to his death the following night, in attempting to escape from Edinburgh Castle by climbing down the rock.

Many historians, notably Pitcairn who in his "Ancient Criminal Trials in Scotland", gave the most detailed account of her condemnation and death, have followed the sympathetic populace in assuming Lady Glamis innocent. But her earlier career does not altogether support the assumption. In 1528 she was summoned before the Estates with three Douglas supporters to answer the charge of "having given assistance to the Earl of Angus in convocating the King's lieges for the invasion of his Majesty's person."[9] Apparently she was found guilty, for in 1531 one Gavin Hamilton had a gift from the Crown of all her goods heritable and moveable. Then in January 1532 she was tried before a Justice Ayre at Forfar for poisoning her husband Lord Glamis, who had died in 1528. She had quarrelled with him for his refusal to bring his following to the support of Angus on that expedition to the Border in 1526 when Scott of Buccleuch attempted the King's rescue. Either Lady Glamis was acquitted or the charge dropped for lack of evidence.[10] However, these details leave little doubt that Lady Glamis was not the persecuted innocent of popular history, but a very forceful woman and a staunch and active member of the house of Douglas. This does not, of course, make her guilty of conspiracy against the King, but it suggests strongly that the accusation against her was not an improbable fabrication. Enmity begets enmity, and it may well be that the implacability of the King towards the Douglases drove them to plan criminal action against him, especially after the hopes held out to them by their agent John Penven had been proved entirely vain.

The sympathy of both contemporary and later writers for the manner of Lady Glamis' death, and their assumption of her innocence, have given rise to the accusation that James V was vindictively cruel. But noblewomen found guilty of either treason or murder were customarily condemned to death by burning; and, given that she was guilty, James did no more than let the law take its course. It may be remembered in this connection that when Anne Boleyn was condemned to death her sentence was that of burning alive or beheading at the King's pleasure; so that, before her beheading, when she said of Henry VIII "a more merciful prince there was never" she had good reason to say so. Again given that Lady Glamis was guilty, the worst that can be said of James V is that he did not show a similar mercy. If she was guilty, his justice was severe; but if he knew her innocent, then indeed he was vindictively cruel.

Even severity, however, was ill-advised, for it could only serve to encourage the growth of sympathy for the Douglases, especially since the guilt of those executed did not command general belief. Besides executing the Master of Forbes and Lady Glamis, James continued to show a completely uncompromising attitude to the exiled members of the Douglas family. According to the historian of the family, Hume of Godscroft, the only Douglas to whom James had ever shown favour, Archibald Douglas of Kilspindie, made a bid to recover his fortunes by returning to Scotland and seeking the King at Stirling. On his arrival he encountered the King riding back to the castle from a hunting expedition. James saw him and remarked to one of his companions "yonder is my Graysteil, Archibald of Kilspindie, if he be alive." As the King approached Kilspindie fell on his knees, but James rode past him without a sign of recognition "and trotted a good round pace up the hill." Kilspindie followed, only to have the castle gates shut in his face. Exhausted after hurrying up the hill of Stirling encumbered by the weight of the "secret", or shirt of mail which he wore beneath his clothes, he sat down on a stone and asked for a drink of water. But since the King had refused to notice him, no one was willing to risk the contagion of disfavour by doing him any service. James subsequently enquired his whereabouts, and expressed displeasure that he had been treated so discourteously, even though he himself had given the example. He then sent Kilspindie a message ordering him to go to France, having remarked that "if he had not taken an oath that no Douglas should ever serve him, he would have received him into his service." Kilspindie went to France where he died, probably in 1540. "This gave occasion to the King of England . . . to blame his nephew, alleging the old saying, 'That a king's face should give grace'."[11]

The "graceless face" readily shown by James V did not endear him to his nobility. He never realized how little he, in common with the Kings of Scots his predecessors, could afford to forfeit the nobility's goodwill. His victories over opposition were too seldom tactfully bargained for, too often brutally enforced. It is perhaps significant that, according to an English ambassador writing in 1536, the King's council consisted of "none else but the papistical clergy"; while as early as 1532 the earls had almost ceased to attend the King's Council, a certain symptom of disaffection. With the clergy James had shown a certain willingness to compromise; the nobility he had subjected to more discipline than they were prepared to endure. His dealings with them achieved nothing but the certainty of future trouble. However, he appeared to be in a very strong position as he prepared for the reception of his second Queen in the spring of 1538.

* * *

In May James sent Lord Maxwell to France to act as his proxy at the marriage, which was performed on the 18th in the Cathedral of Notre Dame in Paris, where, only seventeen months before, James had been present in person to be married to Madeleine. Marie de Guise had digested her disappointment over the English marriage, and if James considered his second Queen inferior to his first he showed it in nothing except perhaps in sending Lord Maxwell to France instead of going himself. François Ier did all possible to make the match a worthy one for the King whom he regarded as his "propre filz": he gave Marie the honorary rank of a Daughter of France, and a dowry of 150,000 *livres*. James could be well satisfied. Furthermore, he had no reason to fear such a disappointment with her appearance as he had experienced over Marie de Bourbon's; he had seen Marie de Guise in France, and remembered her as outstanding among the ladies of François' court.

In a contemporary double portrait of James V and his second Queen, Marie appears as a woman of striking beauty, fine featured and fair skinned with blue eyes and bright red hair. She is shown wearing a dress of crimson and gold brocade, with voluminous ermine sleeves. Between the fingers of her right hand she holds a carnation, symbolic of conjugal fidelity. The King is dressed with equal splendour, in a low cut doublet of cloth of gold bordered with jewels, worn over a white shirt which is gathered into a band of jewels at the neck. Over all he wears a sleeveless black coat, lined and trimmed with white fur. With a gesture which complements the Queen's, he holds an enamelled jewel of St Andrew, which hangs about his neck on a thin gold chain. His colouring is not dissimilar to the Queen's; his skin is as fair as hers, his hair a darker red. He appears as Lesley described him, ". . . of countenance amiable and lovely . . . his eyes grey and sharp." As far as the loveliness of his countenance is concerned, his portraits unanimously testify to his good looks; but to judge by the anecdotes which illuminate his character, his amiability was superficial and intermittent.

However, it was with the greatest amiability and graciousness that James received his new Queen when she landed at Crail on the coast of Fife, on 10th June. He was awaiting her arrival at St Andrews, and as soon as the news of it was brought to him he rode to Crail to meet her, and escorted her back to St Andrews where "the whole lords (i.e. all the lords) both spiritual and temporal, many barons, lairds and gentlemen . . . received the Queen's grace with great honours and merriness, with great triumph and blithness . . ." Sir David Lindsay, foiled by Death of his opportunity to provide a glittering state entry into Edinburgh for Queen Madeleine, had prepared a smaller reception at St Andrews for Queen Marie. At the New Abbey Gate an artificial cloud descended by mechanical contrivance before the Queen, "and opened in two halves instantly, and there appeared a fair lady most like an angel, having the keys of all Scotland in her hands, (and) delivering them to the Queen's grace in sign and token that all the hearts of Scotland were open to the receiving of her grace." Then Sir David Lindsay himself addressed to the Queen a speech "which taught her to serve her God, obey her husband, and keep her body clean according to God's will and commandment" – an early intimation of the sort of speech which Marie's daughter Mary Queen of Scots and grandson James VI would be obliged to endure in post-Reformation Scotland.

The Queen lodged that night in the New Inns of the Abbey, and the following morning "the bishops, abbots, priors, monks, friars and canons regular made great solemnity in the Abbey Kirk with Mass, songs and playing on the organs"; and the blessing of the marriage was performed by David Beaton, as Coadjutor of St Andrews, acting for his uncle the primate who was now a very frail old man. After the ceremony the King returned to St Andrews Castle and the Queen was taken on a tour of the city churches and the colleges of the university. In the words of Pitscottie:

"As soon as the Queen had visited the kirks and colleges and the people and (had) come to her palace and met with the King's grace, she confessed to him she never saw in France nor no other country so many good faces in so little room as she saw that day in Scotland. For she said it was shown to her in France that Scotland was but a barbarous country destitute and void of all commodities that uses to be (i.e. that are in use) in other countries, but now she confessed she saw the contrary . . . At these words of the Queen the King was greatly rejoiced and said to her 'Forsooth, Madam, ye shall see better 'ere ye gang, will God . . .'" (i.e. if God wills).[12]

If the Guise family was not yet the powerful Catholic interest that it became later in the century, Marie de Guise, besides linking the King of Scots in alliance to Catholic France, was herself a strong and orthodox Catholic. If James needed to be influenced in the direction he had already chosen there could be little doubt that Marie would provide that influence. The reformers in Scotland held no such hopes of her as they had held of Queen Madeleine. Furthermore her influence was supported by that of David Beaton, who from 1538 to the end of the reign became increasingly indispensable to James V.

David Beaton had been educated at the universities of Glasgow and St Andrews, possibly Paris and certainly Orléans, and from an early age he had been employed on diplomatic missions in France by the Duke of Albany. According to a kinsman and panegyrist he could easily have been mistaken for a Frenchman. He was always well received at the court of France, and in December 1537, while he was there to negotiate the second marriage of the King of Scots, he was presented to the bishopric of Mirepoix. In the same year he was named successor to his uncle as Archbishop of St Andrews. The following December he became a cardinal, the cardinalate having been requested for him by both François Ier and James V. Possibly he was the type of churchman who has a particular ability to get on with women, for it was François' mother Louise of Savoy who first suggested that he should be given a French benefice; and between him and Marie de Guise a close friendship and political alliance developed. John Knox, who was obsessed by the imagined sexual misdemeanours of his religious and political enemies, attempted to make a scandal out of their relationship. "Howsoever it was before," he wrote, "it is plain that after the King's death, and during the Cardinal's life, whosoever guided the court, he got his secret business sped of that gracious Lady, either by day or by night." However, there is no reason to see in their relations anything but friendship between a civilized and rather lonely Frenchwoman and an urbane and gallicized prelate who had common political interests.

The influence of the Queen and Cardinal Beaton was an additional source of strength to James's already strong personal commitment to the auld alliance and the Catholic Church. But although James supported the Church in Scotland and at the same time relied upon it to support him both politically and financially, he was not unaware of its shortcomings. He could scarcely have remained unaware of them when the majority of his prelates led lives praiseworthy only for their total lack of hypocrisy. Cardinal Beaton, for example, though not the profligate of post-Reformation tradition, was frankly non-celibate. His fidelity to his mistress Marion Ogilvy would have been a creditable quality in a layman and a husband, but it was an irrelevant quality in a churchman who had taken other vows.

Clerical immorality was one source of scandal in the Church, clerical ignorance another. For instance Bishop Crichton of Dunkeld cheerfully admitted to an apostate priest on trial before him in 1539 that he had never read either the Old or the New Testament. "And yet," he said, "thou seest I have come on indifferently well." There was nothing exceptionally scandalous about Crichton's ignorance of the scriptures; the scandalous thing was that it was perfectly normal.

A further contributory cause of the disrepute into which the clergy, especially the bishops, fell was the abuse of "cursing" (i.e. excommunication). Knox remarked that a bishop was willing to sell for a "plak" – a small coin – a letter of excommunication against "all that look over our dyke". A formal letter of excommunication was an awe-inspiring document. In 1525 Archbishop Dunbar had issued a general excommunication against all the disturbers of peace upon the Border – Henderland, Tushielaw, Gilnockie, and their like: –

"I curse their head and all the hairs of their head, I curse their face, their ene (eyes), their mouth, their nose, their tongue, their teeth, their cragis (foreheads), their shoulders, their breasts, their hearts, their stomaches, their backs, their waymes (bellies), their arms, their legs, their hands, their feet, and every part of their bodies from the top of their heads to the sole of their feet, before and behind, within and without; I curse them going, I curse them riding, I curse them standing, I curse them sitting, I curse them eating, I curse them drinking, I curse them waking, I curse them sleeping, I curse them rising, I curse them lying, I curse them at home, I curse them from home, I curse them within the houses, I curse them without the houses, I curse their wives, their bairns and their servants participant with them in their evil and mischievous deeds . . .

". . . the malediction of God that lighten upon Lucifer and all his fellows, that struck them from the heaven to the deep pit of hell, must light upon them (the Borderers) . . . the waters and rivers of Tweed, Teviot, Clyde, Nith, Esk, Ewes and Annan and all other waters where they ride, go or pass must drown them as the Red Sea drowned King Pharaoh and the people of Egypt pursuing God's people of Israel . . .

"I dissever and part them from the kirk of God and deliver them quick (alive) to the devil of hell, there perpetually to remain condemned in body and soul until they convert to God and make amends for their cruel trespasses . . ."[13]

But such words inevitably lost the power of terror when they were too frequently repeated, and especially when, as in the instance of the excommunication quoted, the excommunicated persons remained to all appearance unscathed, until temporal justice dealt with them.

The higher clergy as a whole gave a poor example to the lower, which the lower hastened to follow. Country priests in the main were ignorant and poverty stricken. Frequently they were hated for the pitiless greed with which they exacted their "mortuary dues" from parishioners even poorer than themselves. The mortuary dues, which could be described as death duties paid in kind to the Church, were the "upmost cloth", the coverlet of the dead person's bed, and the "corpse-present beast", usually a cow, which were payable upon burial. A series of deaths could reduce a family to total destitution, but even in such a situation it was seldom indeed that the mortuary dues were unclaimed. While the priests dealt ungenerously with their parishioners they nonetheless sought the same pleasures and fell victim to the same temptations. The lecherous priest and the drunken priest were as commonplace figures of sour mockery as the avaricious priest. Even crime was not unknown. A priest named William Lothian was unfrocked and beheaded for taking part in the murder of James Inglis, Abbot of Culross, in 1531.

Among the prelates Archbishop Dunbar provided a good example of learnedness and holy living; doubtless there were equally good men among the lower clergy, but they were too few. Reform within the Church was unquestionably the first necessity in the successful combating of heresy, for clerical immorality, ignorance, rapacity and crime very obviously played into the hands of the reformers. The churchmen of Scotland may not have been intrinsically worse than their counterparts in the rest of Europe, but as the Reformation had been late in reaching Scotland, so the realization that they must put their house in order and initiate a counter-reformation was late in coming to the Scottish clerics. It came, indeed, too late.

James himself was in a very difficult position with regard to the problem. He was still receiving payments of the £72,000 composition for the "Great Tax", for the collection of which he relied upon the goodwill of his prelates, who had been somewhat grudging in the first place. Moreover he was himself a party to a particularly profitable form of clerical abuse since his bastard sons had been appointed as commendators, or titular abbots of six of the richest abbeys and priories in Scotland. When requesting Pope Paul III to appoint one of his bastards as a commendator James wrote in extenuation of the request "the royal dignity of the boy will put a restraint upon the impious . . ." But he must have known well enough that such a consideration was no more than a slight extenuation of an appointment of this kind. Financially he could not afford either to offend the prelates or to reform the abuses. In consequence he could not play the part of a reforming King with any seriousness of purpose. He fell back upon encouraging anti-clerical satire as a means of stimulating the churchmen to reform themselves.

The first satirist to receive the King's patronage was George Buchanan, who probably came to the King's notice in 1535 when he was in the employ of the Earl of Cassillis.

In that year Buchanan wrote a poem entitled *Somnium*, in which he recounted how St Francis appeared to him in a dream and desired him to become a friar; but Buchanan decided to remain a layman, for that would be the easier way of remaining virtuous – unless St Francis could promise him a bishopric, for which he would be prepared to risk his soul. By 1536 Buchanan had been appointed tutor to the King's eldest bastard son, James Stewart, Abbot of Kelso and Melrose. Thereafter, with the encouragement of the King, he wrote two anti-clerical poems, the *Palinodia*; and at the King's direct command he wrote the *Franciscanus*. In this poem "Who, in the first place," he asks, "are those who become Franciscans? Those ruined in purse, law-breakers, the ignorant, the diseased in mind and body, the used-up gambler and voluptuary. Formerly men when driven to straits committed suicide; now they turn Franciscans."[14] The King's patronage did not serve to prevent the arrest and imprisonment of Buchanan in 1539; happily for him he escaped and fled first to England and subsequently to France.

Buchanan's poems, being written in Latin, though they aroused the fury of the clergy, would have had a fairly limited circulation and impact. The satires of Sir David Lindsay, who wrote in the vernacular, were more widely known and made an influential contribution to the Scottish Reformation. However, Lindsay did not suffer persecution because he did not formally abjure the religion in which he had been born. His attitude to the Church was that of "one of the disgusted faithful."[15] And because he remained a Catholic James was able to give him a protection that he had been unable to extend to Buchanan. With the King's encouragement Lindsay wrote a series of satires. He held clerical immorality up to ridicule in *Kitteis Confessioun*, and savagely attacked the avarice with which the clergy fastened upon the wealth of the dying and the dead in *The Testament of the Papyngo*. But all the sins of commission of which the

Scottish clergy were guilty, and the complete lack of spiritual values which characterized the clerical estate were castigated in *The Satire of the Three Estates*, a dramatic work, a short version of which was performed on Twelfth Night 1540 in the Great Hall of Linlithgow Palace, before the King and Queen and the whole court, including several bishops.

The text of the Linlithgow version of the play has not survived, but its content is known from a detailed account of the performance sent by a pro-English Scot, possibly Thomas Bellenden, a member of the King's council, to Sir William Eure, Captain of Berwick.*

This synopsis incidentally makes no mention of the character of Lady Sensualitie, who appears in the surviving texts of later versions of the play, in which she seduces the King and deflects him from his dutiful preoccupation with the affairs of his kingdom. Lady Sensualitie is traditionally supposed to have represented Margaret Erskine, the Lady of Lochleven. The omission is therefore entirely explicable. Not even Lindsay could have got away with satirizing the King's favourite mistress before the assembled court; but when later versions of the play were performed after the King's death the reputation of the Lady of Lochleven was no longer protected, and Lindsay was free to write in her part as mercilessly as he wished. With his dominating desire for incorruptibility Lindsay would always have seen her in the same simple terms as those in which he portrays Lady Sensualitie – as one of the Vices which appear in mediaeval miracle plays to work the perdition of the human soul.

According to the synopsis, at Linlithgow the play was introduced by the character of *Solace* "who showed first to all the audience the play to be played, which was a general thing, meaning nothing in special to displease no man." The same assurance, perhaps in the same words, is given

* See Appendix B.

James V 'Bonnet Piece'

James V and Marie de Guise

Marie de Guise attributed to Corneille de Lyon

by *Pausa* in one of the surviving versions of the play, as it was presented at Coupar Fife in 1552:

> Prudent people, I pray you all
> Take no man grief in special
> For we shall speak in general
> For passtime and for play.[16]

This assurance given, the Player-King entered surrounded by his courtiers, who addressed to him, and by extension to James V, compliments upon his beauty and his skill in arms. The words addressed by *Flattery* to the Player-King in the later version may perhaps retain the elegant compliment Lindsay offered to James V before proceeding to less digestible matter:

> Now the Virgin Mary save your grace,
> Saw ever man so white a face,
> So great an arm, so fair a hand,
> There is not sic a leg in all this land!
> Were ye in harness* I think no wonder
> Howbeit ye dang down† twenty hunder![17]

The serious business of the play was reached when the character of *Poor Man* entered, asking for the King of Scotland "that hanged John Armstrong with his follows, but had left one thing undone." *Poor Man*, when asked what that was, "made a long narration of the oppression of the poor by the taking of the corpse present beasts, and of the harrying of poor men by consistory law, and of many other abuses of the spirituality . . . Then the Poor Man showed the great abusion of bishops, prelates, abbots, reiving poor men's wives and daughters . . . and of the great superfluous rents that pertained to the Church by reason of overmuch temporal lands given to them . . . and of the great abominable vices that reign in cloisters and of the common bordels that was kept in cloisters of nuns . . ."

* i.e. in arms.   † struck down.

Since the shortcomings of the clergy were already a source of great anxiety to James V he was deeply affected by the *Satire of the Three Estates*. At the close of the performance "The King of Scots did call upon the Bishop of Glasgow being Chancellor and divers other bishops, exhorting them to reform their fashions and manners of living, saying that unless they so did he would send six of the proudest of them unto his uncle of England, and as those were ordered so he would order the rest that would not amend." Archbishop Dunbar answered "that one word of his Grace's mouth should suffice them to be at commandment, and the King hastily and angrily answered that he would gladly bestow any words of his mouth that could amend them . . ."[18]

At the same time as James was taking the only action that he could do to stimulate reform within the Church, Cardinal Beaton took what he considered to be the only effective action for protecting it against Reform from without. Upon his succeeding his uncle as primate in September 1539 he initiated a new phase of persecution. Among those tried before Beaton were several minor clerics and members of religious orders; a vicar and a secular priest, two black friars, a canon regular from the monastery of St Colm's Inch and a grey friar, who was burnt at Glasgow together with a young poet, in spite of the intervention of Archbishop Dunbar who attempted to persuade Beaton to spare their lives. The martyrdoms served only to intensify public sympathy for the reformers' cause and to furnish material for the Protestant hagiography which made influential anti-catholic propaganda in the later phases of the Reformation. The new persecution, though it made few martyrs, caused the flight of many men who might have had to face martyrdom had they remained in Scotland; among them were several distinguished scholars who removed themselves from the dangerous ground of St Andrews to Wittenberg and Leipzig, and also Father Alexander Seton, the King's

Dominican confessor who fled to England. The obvious inference to be drawn from the fact that converts from among the ranks of the clergy were so numerous is that many men who led vigorous spiritual lives were finding fulfilment in the reformed religion, and therefore turning away from the Church rather than giving their efforts to its regeneration. Whatever the solution to this problem, it did not lie in persecution.

James V's encouragement of anti-clerical satire and Beaton's persecution were both directed to the same purpose, that of combating the spread of the Reformation in Scotland. But Henry VIII probably misinterpreted James's intention and assumed him to be entering a personally anti-clerical phase, especially in the light of his outburst at his prelates following the performance of the *Satire of the Three Estates*; for, immediately after this, James came under renewed pressure from England to imitate his uncle's ecclesiastical policy, which Henry hoped would bring the King of Scots' religious position into line with his own. In February 1540 Henry sent Sir Ralph Sadler on embassy to Scotland with instructions to attempt to break the influence of Cardinal Beaton, to urge upon James the advantages of suppressing religious foundations and to impress upon him the value of close alliance with England by hinting at his proximity to the succession.

Sadler wrote the King of England a detailed account of his audiences with King James, and he was unable to conceal the fact that he made little headway.[19] His attempt to procure the disgrace of Beaton was a complete failure, for James was unimpressed by the intercepted letters written by Beaton to his agent in Rome, which Sadler produced to support his statement that the Cardinal was attempting to bring into his own hands, "not only the whole spiritual jurisdiction of your realm, but under colour of it also the temporal . . ." James replied, quite unmoved, that the spiritual jurisdiction was the business of the spirituality and that as far as temporal affairs were concerned no King of Scots had been served more obediently than himself. He did not consider himself anything but his own master. He refused even to read the Cardinal's letters saying "I know not but that he wrote to Rome for the procuring of a legation*, which in good faith should be a benefit to our subjects, and we also did write to the Pope's holiness in the same."[20]

Sadler turned to the matter of ecclesiastical reform in England, and urged upon James a similar policy in suppressing religious houses, by which he would be so greatly enriched that, as Sadler put it, "Ye shall be able to live like a King, and not meddle with sheep." James, who was reputed to have about ten thousand sheep grazing on the crown lands in Ettrick Forest, explained that sheep-farming was the business of his tenant farmers, and added with a regal detachment, "By my truth, I never knew what I had of mine own, nor yet do." As for the suppressing of religious houses "Methinks it is against reason and God's law," he said "to put down thir (i.e. these) abbeys and religious houses, which have stand thir many years, and God's service maintained and keeped in the same. And what need I to take them to increase my livelihood, when I may have anything that I can require of them?"

The King was already receiving so much from the Church that his words to Sadler were by no means an empty boast, and, with the threat that he might follow Henry VIII's example hanging over their heads his churchmen would scarcely be likely to refuse him anything more that he might require. Sadler was indeed trying to press upon him a course of action that had no relevance to the situation in Scotland, for with the commendams held by his bastards James had no need to suppress the religious foundations in order to tap their wealth. Neither would it have benefited him to suppress them for the other purpose to which

* i.e. legatine authority.

Henry VIII had put English church lands, for sale, because very many Scottish abbeys and priories not in the control of the Crown had become unofficially controlled by various noble families. The Chisholms were firmly established in unofficial possession of Dunblane, the Erskines of Dryburgh, the Homes of Jedburgh, the Kennedys of Crossraguel and the Flemings of Whithorn. Sadler, however, was not aware of this situation, and, supposing James to be restrained from following the English example only by his own orthodoxy, he returned to the attack and pleaded the need for reform as a reason for suppressing religious houses. Taking up James's reference to the maintenance of God's service, "I dare be bold to say," he said "that unless your monks be more holy in Scotland than ours are in England, there reigneth nowhere more carnality, incontinency, buggery, sodomy, with lechery, and other abominations than is used in cloisters . . . which could never appear so long as the King's majesty, your uncle, committed his trust to the bishops and clergy of his realm, for their visitations, as your grace now doth." But James was not drawn by this argument either. "Oh," he said, "God forbid that if a few be not good, for them all the rest should be destroyed. Though some be not, there be a great many good; and the good may be suffered and the evil must be reformed, as ye shall hear that I shall help to see it redressed in Scotland, by God's grace, if I brook life."

Perhaps James really supposed that he would be able to initiate a sufficient reform to stem the tide of the Reformation in Scotland; perhaps he did the most human and least effective thing of all — merely hoped for the best.

Sadler was no more successful in pressing upon James a policy of alliance with England. In their relations with each other Henry VIII and James V were principally motivated by fear. James, not without reason, feared Henry's ultimate intention in seeking a close alliance with Scotland: he feared the old claim to suzerainty which Henry had overtly voiced to the herald of James IV in 1513, and had covertly sought to make good during James's own minority. Also, though Henry could scarcely claim suzerainty over the kingdom of a mature sovereign with whom he was nominally at peace, the fact that he persisted "in supporting the infamous Douglases against their sovereign . . . must have rendered his conduct and counsels suspicious, and deservedly to be shunned. He had in a manner forced James to fix a connexion with France."[21] Nonetheless, he feared the auld alliance, especially since a rapprochement between the Emperor and François Ier led him to fear the formation of a Franco-Imperial alliance against himself. Since the link between France and Scotland had become so close, he felt intensely vulnerable to a tripartite league and to the possibility of invasion from the north. Accordingly Sadler was encouraged to woo James with reference to James's proximity to the English succession, particularly in the event of the death of Prince Edward, Henry's only legitimate son, by Jane Seymour. But James was not moved by Sadler's statement that Henry had the power to name his own successor, and that friendly relations might well move him to nominate James: to shape his policy in accordance with such an uncertain eventuality would make him indeed the satellite of England.

In spite of the cool reception given to all his propositions, the ambassador went on to propose a meeting between James and Henry VIII, a proposal which James received courteously and to which he agreed, with the proviso that François Ier should also be present. Yet he was eager to make it plain that he was not the satellite of the European powers, for when Sadler warned him against being made the pawn of the Emperor and the King of France he burst out "I am no bairn, neither Emperor nor French King can draw me to do what they list." Henry VIII, however, with his long political experience, could see that there was a potential vulnerability in James's position as their ally.

In his instructions to Sir Ralph Sadler he had written "To speak of the Emperor or the French King . . . what can he look for at either, or at both their hands, but fair words and entertainment for a time as their instrument *with his own danger** to serve their purposes?" The question was perceptive; the answer was not long withheld.

* author's italics.

Chapter Seven

VAIN GLORY

Our pleasance here is all vain glory
This false world is but transitory . . .
            William Dunbar "Lament for the Makaris"

IN both foreign and domestic policy James V had been consistent throughout his reign. His foreign policy had been consistently pro-Catholic and pro-French. His domestic policy had been consistently authoritarian, aimed at the reduction of violence and the establishment of law and order and effective justice. The College of Justice, for the foundation of which the King has been accorded a generous measure of praise, eventually became a respected and efficient institution; but considering the circumstances of its foundation, this was perhaps rather in spite of the King than because of him. However, he has not perhaps been praised sufficiently for his appointment of an advocate for the poor, an office which had been created in the reign of James I, but had been allowed to lapse. That James V had the interests of his poorer subjects genuinely at heart was shown not only by this measure but also by his attempt to induce the clergy to abolish the hated mortuary dues. In this he was unfortunately unsuccessful. The mortuary dues continued to be levied until the eve of the Reformation rebellion, by which time their abolition was a sop to public opinion offered so late as to be laughably irrelevant. However, James's personal concern for the welfare of his subjects kept him his popularity even though the church which he supported had become the object of public contempt.

According to Lesley the King was "a good and sure justiciar, by the which one thing he allured to him the hearts of all the people, because they lived quietly and in rest, out of all oppression and molestation of the nobility and rich persons."[1]

In the year 1539 there was a resurgence of internal disorder, with the rebellion of Donald Gorme of Sleat, who had a hereditary claim to the Lordship of the Isles, which had for so long maintained an existence almost independent of the Crown of Scotland. Donald Gorme was killed while laying siege to Eilean Donan Castle. His rebellion had been abortive, but obviously it was the fact that it had occurred at all, and had been occasioned by the revival of the ancient claim, which decided James V to make an expedition in person to secure the peace and ensure the obedience of the northern parts of his realm. In the spring of 1540 he planned and prepared a naval expedition to circumnavigate the north of Scotland. The Queen was pregnant, and James awaited the birth of the child before sailing. The child was the hoped-for Prince, who was given the royal name of James. He was "fair and lifelike to succeed us," as the King jubilantly informed Henry VIII on the day of his birth, 22nd May.[2]

In great rejoicing the King set sail from Leith on 29th May. He was accompanied by Cardinal Beaton, the Earls of Huntly and Arran and by his favourite, Oliver Sinclair, who, in the course of the voyage, he appointed Sheriff of Orkney, and during the year, governor of Tantallon Castle.

The voyage had the nature both of a warlike expedition and of a royal progress. There were twelve ships, which were heavily equipped with artillery, but on board the King's ship his own living quarters were luxuriously furnished. During the voyage he ate to the sound of music and was served upon gold plate, for since he was on a progress it was important for reasons of prestige that he should be surrounded by splendour. Accounts of the progresses of François Ier, and of course Pitscottie's account of the Earl of Atholl's entertainment of James V, carefully stress the point that on progress the King was lodged with as much splendour as if he were in one of his own palaces. The *grands seigneurs* of France in their "greniers", and the entourage of James V, under hatches, had to endure discomforts that they would never have tolerated at home; the purpose of their presence on a progress was solely to enhance the prestige of the sovereign. In this context it is obviously significant that James's companions were his minister Cardinal Beaton, his personal friend Huntly, his near kinsman Arran, and his favourite Sinclair. Those lords who were disaffected, or at least out of sympathy with the King, were not prepared to participate in the hardships of the voyage which would have been their lot.

James V's expedition sailed northward, following the coastline of Fife. It passed the little port of Crail, where James had received his second Queen, rounded Fife Ness, and sailed on past St Andrews, where so recently he had made that second marriage which seemed so much more auspicious than the first. In 1540 the most impressive landmark of St Andrews, the tower of St Regulus, did not stand out so bleakly as it stands to-day: then the abbey and the nearby Castle still stood intact, two magnificent groups of buildings, the realities and the symbols of spiritual and temporal power.

The King's fleet sailed on, crossed the Firth of Tay, and continued its northward course past Arbroath, a very small township which clung about the walls of the great red sandstone abbey, where in the circular window of the south transept, "the Round O of Arbroath", there shone a lantern which did duty for a lighthouse. The voyage continued past the Castle of Dunottar, impregnably perched upon its massive rock, and past Aberdeen, which was possibly the most northerly place in his kingdom which James had previously visited. The expedition rounded Kinnaird Head, crossed the Moray Firth, and continued along the shores of Caithness. The King landed in Caithness, before continuing his voyage, across the Pentland Firth, to Orkney.

He reached the seas in which lie those groups of islands that comprised the northernmost extremity of his kingdom, the islands of Orkney and Shetland, at the time of year when darkness never wholly falls, and when the hours of night are hours of a luminous dusk known as the "simmer dim". A late-sixteenth century poet thought himself, in Orkney, to be

> "Upon the utmost corners of the world,
> And on the margins of this massive round . . ."

But James was both pleased and somewhat surprised to find these remote, half-Scandinavian islands, the most recent acquisition of the Crown of Scots, both more prosperous and better ordered than he had expected. Thus gratified he returned once more to the mainland. When the expedition again put to sea, it doubled Cape Wrath and made for the Isle of Lewis. The second half of the voyage had begun.

The King visited Lewis and Harris and North and South Uist, where, as an eighteenth century historian charmingly put it, "The distant and lawless inhabitants . . . rushed from their muddy hovels to gaze upon the lion of Scotland." James next landed on the Isle of Skye, where the name of the principal town commemorates his visit. Portree is a corruption of the Gaelic name meaning "King's Haven" which it was given in his honour. He then sailed on, to land upon Coll, Tiree and Mull, and the mainland coast of Argyll. Thereafter the expedition rounded the long promontory of Kintyre, and visited Arran and Bute, before bringing the King and his entourage to the end of their voyage at Dumbarton, towards mid-August.

While the King's fleet had followed that eastern coastal strip of Scotland which is spiritually and geographically lowland, the expedition had maintained the character of a progress. Upon the second half of the voyage the heavy artillery of the royal ships had shown its purpose, which was to overawe the unruly and the potentially rebellious. When the King landed in Sutherland, upon the Western Isles, and on the West Coast, he had seized and borne away captive a number of chieftains whose loyalty he doubted, or had taken hostages from among their relatives. In Sutherland he had seized Donald Mackay of Strathnaver, and in Lewis Roderick Macleod and his principal kinsmen. In Skye he had taken Alexander Macleod of Dunvegan and also John Moydertach, the Captain of Clan Ranald, and Alexander of Glengarrie, who were of "Maconeyllis kin", i.e. relatives of the rebel Donald Gorme of Sleat. He had also seized John Mackenzie, Chief of the Clan Mackenzie, Hector Maclean of Duart and James Macconel of Islay.[3] The captives and hostages were all landed at Dumbarton, and the ships and their crews then reversed their course and returned to Leith.

In addition to its disciplinary purpose the King's voyage was also of navigational value, for the pilot, Alexander Lindsay, made charts of the coastal waters and kept detailed notes of the various hazards to be encountered in voyaging there. Lindsay's notes were translated into French by Nicholas de Nicolay, Seigneur d'Arfeuille, Cosmographer to Henry II of France, and were printed in the form of a tract entitled "La Navigation du Roy d'Ecosse, Jacques V". Later editions of d'Arfeuille's work somehow acquired the title of "La Vie et la Mort de Jacques V", which was less than justified, for the work deals only with the voyage of 1540, and is concentrated entirely upon its navigational aspects.

The Parliament which met in December 1540 enacted what had been the main political result of the expedition, the annexation of the Lordship of the Isles to the Crown of Scotland. It also enacted the confirmation of the revocation

164

of all grants made during the King's minority. The original revocation had been made, in accordance with Scottish practice, on the King's twenty-fifth birthday, which had occurred while he was in France, on 10th April 1537. The practice of making a revocation was inevitably unpopular with the nobility since it caused them to disgorge what they had come to regard as their own, but James V's revocation was especially unpopular, since with his aptitude for seizing every opportunity of financial advantage he used it "as an instrument to exact large sums by way of compositions."[4]

However, James did not use this Parliament only to make personally advantageous enactments. It also legislated against the spread of heresy and, ominously, against the spread of iconoclasm. This particular measure shows that by this date the Reformation had ceased to be an intellectual movement and had become a popular one, against which mere legislation would prove ineffectual. This Parliament, in an attempt to ensure the efficacy of its legislation, ruled that henceforth the acts of parliament should be printed, that thereafter no one could plead ignorance of them. However, this act was itself ineffectual, possibly due to the sheer technical difficulty of what it demanded, for no volume of printed acts was issued until 1566.

At the beginning of the new year the Queen was again pregnant, and now that she had proved herself so amply James gave her a belated coronation. A crown was made for her by James Mosman the royal goldsmith, at least partially of gold from the mines of Crawford Muir, which were being productively worked by miners from Lorraine, brought to Scotland upon the Queen's initiative. For himself James had the exquisite gothic crown worn by his father and grandfather refashioned as an imperial crown, arched and surmounted by a cross set with pearls, in which form the Crown of Scots has survived unaltered. James's choice of an imperial crown may have been influenced by Henry

VIII's claim to "imperial" power over his dominions; James's probable intention was to make visually clear the independence of Scotland from Henry's "empire". François Ier had made a similar gesture, by converting the Crown of France from a gothic diadem into an arched imperial crown, to illustrate the independence of the French Crown from the Holy Roman Empire.

At the opening of the year 1541 James V appeared to have reached the apogee of his achievement and his prosperity. He seemed strong in his alliance with France. The succession seemed doubly assured with the birth of a second prince, Arthur, in April. The King seemed to have established peace and order within his kingdom, though the spread of the Reformation admittedly threatened the King's peace. Lastly, and with unquestioned success, he had overcome the poverty in which he had found the Crown at the beginning of his personal rule, and in Lesley's words had "wonderfully enriched" himself and his realm. He had, at least, wonderfully enriched himself.

After his return from France James not only continued to amass wealth, but also began to spend lavishly – too lavishly, perhaps. Evidently he had derived enormous inspiration from his visit to France, for according to Lesley "there was many new 'ingynis' and devices, as well of building of palaces, habiliments, as of banquetting and of men's behaviour, first begun and used in Scotland at this time, after the fashion which they had seen in France. Albeit it seemed to be very comely and beautiful, yet it was more superfluous and voluptuous nor (than) the sustenance of the realm of Scotland might bear forth or sustain . . ."

In an age when princes were greatly concerned with the magnificence of their image in the public eye, James had seen and fallen under the influence of the most magnificent of all the princes of the time, François Ier. Without doubt James wished to make the image of the Crown of Scots measure up as well as possible to the more glorious image

of the Crown of France. The refashioning of the regalia
served this purpose, as well as that of asserting the independence of the Scottish Crown from the "empire" of England.
Not only the crown was refashioned but also the sceptre,
which like the crown has survived unaltered in the form which
was given it by James V. It has a silver-gilt shaft with an
elaborate gold head, decorated with figurines of Our Lady,
St Andrew and St James, and supporting a sphere of rock
crystal which in turn is topped by a gold finial containing
a Scottish pearl. Shortly before he ordered the refashioning
of the regalia James issued a very beautiful new coinage
which showed a great artistic advance upon the earlier
coinages of the reign. The gold ducats or "bonnet pieces"
of 1539 were current for two pounds and were minted in
Scottish gold.[5] They bear an elegant likeness of James V,
in profile, and wearing a flat bonnet instead of the crown
as was conventional in representing the sovereign on the
coinage. More startling, however, than the unconventional
image is the gauntness of the King's face, for he was still
in his twenties.

Besides the enhancement of the King's image a further
sign of the influence of the French visit was the enlargement
and elaboration of the royal household which took place
after James had seen the splendour which surrounded
his father-in-law. The household became increasingly
expensive to maintain, too expensive, indeed, for the
resources of the Crown; £10,000 a year of the clerical
taxation was diverted to meet the cost.[6]

One small innovation directly traceable to French
influence was the introduction to Scotland of the consort
of viols. As an instrument the viol was already known in
Scotland, for one Richard Hume, an "Inglishmanne",
was given £20 to buy materials to "mak violis to the Kingis
grace" in 1535. But in France James first heard a consort
consisting of two trebles, a tenor and a bass viol, and after
his return the employment of four "violars" in his household

strongly suggests that James employed them as a consort in the French fashion.[7] For his own music making, however, the King's favourite instrument continued to be the lute.

Personal splendour and the increased expense of the household accounted for a considerable proportion of the King's expenditure, but his most lavish spending was upon an ambitious programme for the architectural embellishment of the royal palaces, especially Falkland and Stirling. A certain amount of building work had been done before the King's visit to France, for "all the royal castles and palaces were repaired and put in good order in anticipation of the King's marriage in 1537".[8] But the work done between 1537 and the end of the reign was done with the intention of making the royal residences of Scotland worthy of comparison with those of France.

James V inherited a group of essentially mediaeval residences, on which a certain amount of improvement and expansion had been begun during his father's reign. But the work started by James IV had been cut short by the disaster of Flodden, and though the Duke of Albany had continued the improvements in progress at Holyrood for his own convenience, for the most part the work done during James V's minority had been merely the necessary work of maintenance. Therefore when James V turned his attention to the improvement of his palaces, he found a certain amount of relatively recent reconstruction had been undertaken which served very well as a basis upon which his own principally decorative ideas could be carried out.

The Master of Works who had been in charge of what was done before the King's marriage was John Scrymgeour of Myres, who held office from about 1529 to about 1562; but the improvements undertaken between 1537 and 1540 seem to have been entrusted principally to Sir James Hamilton of Finnart. If Finnart had never wholly recovered the favour of the King after displeasing him so profoundly in 1536, James at least continued to appreciate his taste, his knowledge of architecture and his organizing ability. He was first employed in charge of building works at Linlithgow in 1535, and then, in association with Scrymgeour at Stirling. On 9th September 1539 he was appointed "Master of Werk principale to our soverane lord of all his werkis within his realme, now biggand or to be biggit (now in building or to be built), and to haif thre or four deputis under him, quha sall answer to him and his directioun owerall."[9] His salary was £200 a year. To him are attributed the most remarkable architectural monuments of the reign of James V. Yet his actual tenure of the office of Master of Works was very short, for he fell finally from grace in 1540. So it may be that more credit than is usually allowed them should be given to his deputies, who continued to exercise their duties until the end of the reign.

At Linlithgow the Master Mason was one Thomas French, who received a salary of £40 a year "gratis Ja. Hamilton". At Falkland one John Brownhill was employed as Master Mason from 1537 to 1541, and a Frenchman named Nicholas Roy who also received an appointment as Master Mason during the King's pleasure was employed there between 1539 and 1541.[10]

At Falkland James V had inherited the keep of a mediaeval castle, and a great hall built by James III, to which James IV had added two new ranges of buildings. The great hall formed the north range of an intended quadrangle, and there had been added an east range and a south range. The south range possessed a great gate house, its entry flanked by two towers with conical roofs. This was completed in James IV's reign. The rest of the south range of buildings remained uncompleted, and provided the groundwork for James V's improvement. The courtyard façade of this south range has five elegantly proportioned windows each flanked by a pair of carved stone medallions representing mythological personages, traditionally supposed to be likenesses of James V, his two Queens and his principal courtiers. This improvement was indeed "a Renaissance screen which hangs in front of an unaffected Gothic range a corridor's breadth behind . . . a two-dimensional exercise in Renaissance design."[11] yet it has also been described as "the finest monument to the auld alliance" and "a display of early Renaissance architecture without parallel in the British Isles."[12]

At Stirling likewise James V inherited a late mediaeval fortress, substantially the work of James III, whose architect had built there a great hall, a gatehouse and a chapel royal. James IV had begun a palace block to contain new royal apartments. This building was completed under James V's programme, and the result is a curious mixture of late mediaeval structure and Renaissance ornament. "The battlemented parapet and the crow-stepped gable surmounted grandly by a lion sejant supporting a crown . . . are quite mediaeval. But the detail is not. The winged faces and the panels of thin foliage on square columns are straight from the Renaissance repertory . . . The parapet which oversails the wall face is supported by a cornice inhabited by cheerful winged angel-faces, not Gothic at all but putti from France or Italy . . . These energetic sculptures are obviously derivative. The source is less obvious. Posed and posturing within Gothic wall arches . . . they perversely suggest Blois and the work of François Ier . . ."[13] This inspiration is not surprising, for James V had stayed at Blois in the autumn of 1536 and there had signed his contract of marriage to the Princess Madeleine.

At Linlithgow James V, adding on to buildings dating from the two preceding reigns, completed the palace to surround a central quadrangle.[14] James V's south facade has a graceful range of five high, narrow windows belonging to the chapel, and the fine porch of the "inner entrie" which once had the royal arms carved above the door. To the pre-1537 period of his works belongs the outer entry, over which were displayed the insignia of the Golden Fleece, the

St Michael and the Garter. The armorial carvings now displayed above the outer entry are nineteenth century replacements. The insignia of the Order of the Thistle, which was founded in the reign of James VII and II, were then added.

At Holyrood James V built on to the James IV Tower, completed by his father, a long range of buildings containing a privy chamber, presence chamber, guard hall and chapel. "This gave the royal residence an important architectural façade facing the west, in the centre of which was the main entrance flanked by engaged rounds containing large windows."[15] Unhappily the James V façade was damaged shortly after the King's death during the Earl of Hertford's invasion of Scotland in 1544; and it was ultimately demolished in 1676 and replaced when the palace was rebuilt for King Charles II. James V also built an outer gateway which was demolished in 1755, so that of the four royal palaces Holyrood is the one which has least to show of the works of James V. At the end of his reign, however, James's palaces were "all invested with a stylistic panache which was quite new"[16].

Money for this building programme had come from three sources: the Three Teinds, the Great Tax, and an extra-ordinary tax voted by the Estates on 12th June 1535 to meet the expenses incurred by James himself and his ambassadors during negotiations for his marriage.[17] Since François Ier ultimately paid the whole cost of James's visit to France, this money was free to be expended on the embellishment of the palaces.

The interiors of James's palaces matched the exteriors in elegance and splendour, but of this the evidence is even less complete. At Falkland the ceilings of the royal apartments were repainted in 1537 by an artist whose colours included azure, vermilion, indigo and "much fine gold."[18] Of the sixteenth century painted ceilings nothing remains. Only the King's bedchamber has a newly constructed timber ceiling painted with heraldic decorations embodying the thistle, the saltire, the fleur-de-lis and the cross of Lorraine, which is intended to recreate the appearance which the room would have had during the last years of James V's reign.

Something more remains of the interior of Stirling, where the ceiling of the King's presence chamber was decorated with a set of fifty-six carved medallions, the famous "Stirling Heads", of which thirty-eight survive. The ceiling, having become unsafe, was taken down in 1777, but the surviving medallions, having undergone many vicissitudes, are to be replaced in their original position.*

Medallions, upon ceilings as at Stirling or upon walls as at Falkland, medallions of wood, stone or terra cotta, were frequently introduced into the decorative schemes of Renaissance buildings. Most often the medallion was composed of a portrait head or bust surrounded by a circular garland of flowers or fruit or foliage. Some of the "Stirling Heads", however, are not heads at all: two of them are garlanded figures of naked *putti*, one is a humorously conceived figure of a court fool, clad in traditional motley and bells; one is a vigorous representation of Samson and the lion. But in this series of medallions by far the greater number comprise heads, busts or half-lengths. An eighteenth century visitor to Stirling wrote "in the roof of the Presence Chamber, are carv'd the heads of the Kings and Queens of Scotland", a supposition which has been endlessly repeated and has given rise to futile attempts to fit an identity to each medallion. The traditional identification of one of them as James V has persisted. Another, it has been suggested, may represent Margaret Tudor. The James medallion shows a man who bears a vaguely discernible resemblance to the portraits and coins of James V. He wears a bonnet similar to that shown in most representations of the King, and his hair is concealed by a "caul" which would

* At the time of writing (April 1971) they are on exhibition at Stirling Castle, prior to their replacement.

perhaps have been woven of gold wire or metallic thread, a fashion which does not appear in any of the authenticated likenesses of James V. The Margaret Tudor medallion shows a woman who wears a pedimented English hood, and carries a little greyhound. The tentative identification is based on the fact that the greyhound was one of the Tudor family emblems. But in all probability the "Stirling Heads" represent mythological personages, some of whom may have been carved in the likenesses of the King and his courtiers, as is supposed to have been the case with the medallions on the façade of the south range at Falkland.

Besides the permanent decorations, such as carvings or paintings on walls and ceilings, the royal apartments also contained moveable furnishings to enhance both their beauty and comfort. Tapestries, hangings, counterpanes and bed curtains accompanied the King from one palace to the next. James V possessed many tapestries, mostly French and Flemish, amongst which was one series depicting "The Creation of the World", and others illustrating the "Story of Susanna", the "Story of Troy", the "Story of Æneas" "Hercules", "The Unicorne", and so on. A series entitled "The Story of the Tryumphant Dames" was bought in Paris in 1538. Five pieces of tapestry illustrating the story of Æneas are now hanging in the Palace of Hampton Court; these are possibly tapestries which once graced the palaces of James V, transported to England by his grandson, James VI and I. [19]

*　　*　　*

Occupied with the creation of splendour to surround himself and to give a visible expression to the greatness of the Crown of Scots, James V must have appeared powerful, prosperous and fortunate. But there was much below this impressive surface that threatened the security of his position.

The King was not in good health. In the summer of 1537 he had had a hunting accident in Stirling Park, and though at the time he had made light of the hurts that he sustained it is possible that he was injured more seriously than he himself or anyone else realized. From that time onwards his health began to deteriorate. Quite large sums of money began to be spent on obtaining medicines for him from abroad, and a reference to some unspecified illness occurs in a letter written by James to Marie de Guise, probably some time in 1540, and evidently in response to a complaint which she had made of his absence. "I have received the letter which it pleased you to write to me," he wrote. "I found it very strange, being ill as I have been for these three days past."[20]

Recently much publicity has been given to the theory that Mary, Queen of Scots suffered from and passed on to some of her descendants the rare, hereditary disease of porphyria. The possibility should perhaps be taken into consideration that her father James V may also have suffered from this disease; but since evidence of the exact nature of his illness is completely lacking there is no means of investigating this possibility. Furthermore, until 1537, to all appearances James had enjoyed excellent health. Injuries resulting from his hunting accident seem to offer the only clue to the decline of his health after that date.

To a gradually increasing burden of physical illness was added the burden of nervous stress as the difficulties of his position intensified. James had begun to be on uneasy terms with his nobility as early as 1530, and the deterioration of his relations with them was continuous and was accelerated by a startling event of the late summer of 1540: the final disgrace and execution of Hamilton of Finnart.

In August, shortly after the King's return from his northern voyage, Sir James Hamilton of Kincavel, Sheriff of Linlithgow, denounced Hamilton of Finnart, with whom he was at feud, for plotting against the King's life and for holding treasonable communication with the Douglases. The circumstances of the denunciation were dramatic.

James was waiting upon the south shore of the Forth for a
boat which was to take him across into Fife, when he was
approached by Kincavel's son who told him that Finnart
"attended only the occasion when he might surprize him"
and "breaking up his chamber doors assassinate him."
The mention of communication with the Douglases, and
"the accusation being given by a cousin of the subject,
against a family which a little disorder in the state might
turn successors to the Crown", impressed the King. He
gave Kincavel's son a ring to show to the members of his
council who were in Edinburgh, which should signify his
authority to assemble in his absence, arrest Finnart and
bring him to trial. He was arrested by Sir Thomas Erskine
of Haltoun, Sir James Learmont, Master of the Household,
and Sir William Kirkcaldy of Grange, the Treasurer. Since
Finnart had been notoriously "terrible and cruel against
all whom he could overreach", they risked no delay and no
change of heart in the King, but hastily brought Finnart
to trial and found him "guilty of such points of the indict-
ment as was laid against him."[21] It is also said that he demanded trial by combat with his accuser, and was worsted.
At all events, he was sentenced to death, and died protesting
his innocence of any conspiracy against the King.

It transpired that he had indeed murdered the Earl of
Lennox after the battle of Linlithgow in 1526, for he had
been paying six priests to "do suffrage for the soul of the
deceased John, earl of Lennox, for seven years, three of
them to sing continually in the College Kirk of Hamilton,
and the other three to sing continually in the Black Friars
of Glasgow."[22] The seven years had run out by the time of
Finnart's death, but the King renewed the arrangement,
paying the priests from Finnart's forfeited estates.

Though Finnart had been intensely unpopular his execution shocked the nobility very much more than had the
executions of the Master of Forbes and Lady Glamis. Like
them he was generally believed to have been innocent of the

crime for which he died. But they had always been objects of suspicion and dislike to the King as relatives of Angus, whereas Finnart had once been the King's favourite, and latterly had been of value to him as Master of Works. If the King would execute such a man as Finnart who could regard his life as safe? Many concluded that the King's real motive for putting him to death had been covetousness, the more so as among Finnart's forfeited possessions the King acquired a hoard of gold. To covetousness, it was reported in 1539, the King inclined "daily more and more."[23] Doubtless he was driven to it as his household expenses and his building works ate up the money from the clerical taxation diverted to pay for them. Either the money was insufficient for the purpose or else the expenditure left the King feeling that it had depleted his resources too much. To recoup them, he resorted to some dubious forms of extortion. The 8th Earl of Crawford, whose son "the Wicked Master" the King compelled to resign succession to the earldom, was mulcted of large sums; and the 3rd Earl of Morton was "relentlessly harried" until he agreed to resign his lands to his kinsman Sir William Douglas of Lochleven, Margaret Erskine's husband, who made them over to the King.[24]

It was therefore little wonder that the King became increasingly alienated from his nobility, and derived from the realization of that situation a desperate sense of insecurity. According to Drummond, after the execution of Hamilton of Finnart many of the nobility left the court "which made the King suspicious of them, and believe they favoured the reformed religion, and preferred the friendship of King Henry his uncle to his. Neither was he herein far mistaken." In his anxiety, by day "he turned so retired, sullen and melancholy that everything displeased him, and he became even insupportable to himself." By night his anxieties "limned their dark shadows of displeasures, which gave him terrible affright in his sleep." In other words he began to suffer from depression and from nightmares;

and inevitably, in the light of the theories concerning dreams which were then current, the King's nightmares were assumed to be caused by guilt over the unjust execution of Finnart. Buchanan tells that among the King's nightmares "there was one more remarkable than the rest, which was much talked of, that, in his sleep, he saw James Hamilton running at him with his drawn sword; and that he first cut off his right arm, then his left, and threatened him shortly to come and take away his life." This nightmare came to be endued with particular significance as a result of the great misfortune that shortly afterwards befell the King.

In April 1541 the Prince James who was aged eleven months, fell suddenly ill at St Andrews. The King, who was at Linlithgow when he received the news, rode hard to St Andrews and arrived to find the Prince already dead. And there, to the grief-stricken King news was brought that the new-born Prince Arthur had fallen dangerously ill in Stirling Castle. James rode at once to Stirling, and on his arrival found the younger prince dead also. The two princes were buried together at Holyrood, and it was said that there was more general grief in Scotland over their deaths than there had been rejoicing for their births. They, according to the quasi-biblical dream interpretation of the period, were the right arm and the left arm of the King's dream. James was not perhaps immune from the superstitious terrors attendant upon the obvious interpretation of the conclusion of the dream. His anguish of mind was so great that the Queen controlled her own grief and endeavoured to offer him comfort. "They were young enough," she is reported to have said "and God would send them more succession."

The King forced himself to go on with his usual activities. In the summer of 1541 he and the Queen, black-clad in mourning for their children, went on a northern progress, in the course of which they were ceremonially received at Aberdeen where they stayed fifteen days and were entertained by the students of the university with plays, and with Greek and Latin orations to which both of them probably listened with more courteous attention than comprehension. They journeyed south once more to receive an English ambassador, again Sir Ralph Sadler, who had been sent to Scotland to revive the proposal that a meeting should take place between James V and Henry VIII, on English ground.

When Henry had sent Sadler on embassy to Scotland in 1540 he had been in fear of the previously mentioned *rapprochement* between François Ier and the Emperor, who in 1538 had signed the Treaty of Nice, engineered by Pope Paul III. Subsequently the Emperor and the French King had met on board ship in the harbour of Aigues-Mortes, and François Ier had given the Emperor a diamond ring as a pledge of eternal friendship. Their ancient rivalry for the present put aside, they planned a joint crusade against heresy, which included heretical England. In December of that year the Pope launched his bull of excommunication and deposition against Henry VIII which had been drawn up in 1535. The immediate pretext for the promulgation of the bull was Henry's destruction of the great shrine of St Thomas Becket at Canterbury, an act of sacrilege that outraged Catholic Europe. The Pope's intention was to bring about a coalition of the Emperor, the French and the Scots against the heretical King of England. From this moment Henry began military preparations. Coastal defences were put in order, ready to repel invasion from Europe, and a military build-up began along the Border in readiness to resist invasion from Scotland. When Sadler arrived in August 1541 Cardinal Beaton was on embassy in France. His purpose, it was supposed, was to procure "the extirpation of heresy from Scotland and the re-establishment of the Catholic faith within the dominions of Henry VIII, by a coalition between Francis, James, the emperor and the papal see"[25] — in other words to unite the European powers to take action upon the previous diplomacy of the Pope. By this time, however, the eternal friendship of François and the Emperor was proving to be but transitory. Their habitual rivalry had begun to reassert itself. The Emperor was planning an expedition against Algiers, which sailed and proved a fiasco in the autumn; François, whose diplomacy was always more unorthodox than the Emperor's, was negotiating with the Turks. As ever, the struggle between them was a matter of *realpolitik*, crusades against this or that an ideal to which they paid lip-service. Scotland and England, the peripheral powers, came in on either side according to the exigencies of their own affairs. In 1541 Henry VIII still feared the possibility of becoming the victim of a tripartite alliance; when that fear was removed he sided with the Emperor against the aggression of François Ier. James V feared English aggression, and most probably had sent Beaton to France not to urge military action against England but to appeal for help in the event of invasion. When rivalry between François and the Emperor was resumed James remained true to the auld alliance. War between England and Scotland was on the verge of being brought about by mutual fear and by international alignments.

While the outcome of Beaton's mission to France was still in doubt, Henry VIII was playing for time. So was James. Henry, while increasing his military power in the north, invited James to meet him at York. James, while awaiting Beaton's return, agreed. It is not improbable that James had no intention of risking his person on English ground, but he allowed Henry to make the journey to York – the most northerly journey that the King of England made in the whole course of his reign – and there he left him to wait for twelve days. It was reported that James's clerical counsellors had refused to let him go to England in case the persuasions of his uncle should induce him to embrace the Reformation. Henry, believing this, scornfully remarked "We would be loathe to put him to so great pains (i.e. as to go to York), seeing he cannot without leave of others do it." But James himself made a Border incident for which he demanded redress the excuse for not attending the interview, which he refused to do unless or until redress was obtained.[26] Henry, enraged by the public humiliation of awaiting the King of Scots without result, journeyed south to be greeted in England with the revelation of the infidelities of his fifth Queen, Catherine Howard, who was duly executed. Henry was in an intolerant mood as the year 1541 drew to its end. He had no doubt that James intended trouble, whether as a member of a European coalition or as the ally of France.

The death of Margaret Tudor, the princess whose marriage to James IV had been intended to cement a perpetual peace between Scotland and England, though irrelevant to the situation of 1541, served to symbolize the end of the uneasy peace which had existed between the two countries throughout the reign of her son. In 1540 she had spoken her own epitaph to Sir Ralph Sadler when she said "Though I be forgotten in England, I shall never forget England." It was because she had never forgotten England sufficiently to take the affairs of her adoptive country to heart that Margaret had received and deserved so little honour in Scotland. It is a well known story that when Henry VII had first sought to marry his daughter to James IV one of his councillors suggested the danger of England's becoming a province of Scotland, whereupon Henry VII had dismissed the idea with the words "No, the smaller will ever follow the larger kingdom." It was no doubt with this in mind that Henry VIII, when told of his sister's death, remarked that few Kings of Scots had married English princesses, and that he was sorry that this marriage had taken no better effect.

At the beginning of 1542 Henry had resolved to rectify that lack of effect. He decided to invade Scotland rather than wait upon James's intentions, whatever they might be; and in April, as a preliminary to invasion, he ordered the Archbishop of York "To make a search into the most ancient records and muniments within his diocese so as to ascertain his title to the Kingdom of Scotland."[27]

In the meantime Henry considered a proposal by Sir Thomas Wharton, the governor of Carlisle, that the King of Scots should be kidnapped on Scottish soil, thus saving King Henry much expenditure of money and lives. Henry entertained the proposal, but his Privy Council to which he submitted it had sufficient reverence for the person of a sovereign to react with horror. Henry therefore went forward with his intention to extend his authority over Scotland by the more orthodox method of straightforward militarism.

From April onwards events led swiftly to the outbreak of war. Cardinal Beaton had returned from France without having gathered the continental powers into a crusade against England. The moment for doing so (if it had ever existed in anything except the lip service paid by Catholic sovereigns to the idea of a crusade against heresy) had passed. He had not even obtained a promise of French support against English invasion; François was too heavily engaged with preparations to make war upon the Emperor. As in the past the auld alliance would operate in the favour of France. Henry VIII was proposing to make war on France as the ally of the Emperor; James, like his father before him, was cast in the part of the ally of France. A situation something like that of 1513 had come again, but this time Henry, expecting the traditional "stab in the back" when he went to war in France, intended to stab first.

An unofficial state of war on the Borders preceded an official one, and each King accused the other of having provided a *casus belli*. But on 24th August 1542 Sir Robert Bowes, captain of Norham Castle and English Warden of the East March, invaded Scotland with a troop of 3,000 horse. He was accompanied by the Earl of Angus and Sir George Douglas. The Earl of Huntly, however, had a force ready to meet them and they were soundly defeated at Haddon Rig, near Kelso. Huntly took 600 prisoners, amongst whom was Sir Robert Bowes. Angus and his brother, fortunately for themselves, escaped.

Haddon Rig was the prelude to full-scale war. King Henry ordered the Duke of Norfolk to levy an army of 40,000 men for the invasion of Scotland. Norfolk went to York accompanied by the Earls of Southampton, Shrewsbury, Rutland, Derby, Cumberland and Hertford, and by Angus, who even under these circumstances was following the wayward tradition of his family and thinking not as a Scot but as a Douglas. At York, however, Norfolk and his subordinates were met by Scottish commissioners sent by James to attempt to negotiate a truce.

The King of Scots was in a state of desperate anxiety, for though the country faced invasion there was no unanimity among the lords. James first showed his anxiety by quite unjustly accusing Huntly of not having made the most of his victory, and relieving him of his command, which he gave to the Earl of Moray. Scarcely knowing upon whom he could rely, James discovered the probability that he would have to pay a heavy price for his high-handed treatment of his nobility in the past. He was now obliged to look for the support of a group of men many of whom had at one time or another suffered disfavour or imprisonment, some of whom had suffered from his covetousness or who feared it, some of whom favoured the principles of the Reformation, and some of whom sympathized with the Douglases. On the Burgh Muir of Edinburgh James mustered an army of 30,000 men, but it was an army full of division and unrest, in no way resembling the enthusiastic host which had followed James IV to Flodden: and since that host had been defeated, what better result could James V expect?

No truce delayed Norfolk, who invaded Scotland and made a tour of the Borders looting, spoiling and burning.

His invasion was backed by Henry VIII's claim, made on 5th November, to suzerainty over Scotland.[28] James, knowing that he could expect no help from François who was now at war with the Emperor, appealed to the Pope, declaring that Henry was only making war upon him because he would not desert the Holy See or make war upon the King of France.[29] Norfolk, however, was fighting a campaign fraught with difficulties. His army was badly victualled and his soldiers grew disaffected when supplies of beer ran short. Having done as much damage as possible Norfolk retired to his own side of the Border.

In the meantime James with a much more seriously disaffected army was marching south. He encamped on Fala Muir, a plateau near the western end of the Lammermuir hills; and it was here that the discovery of Norfolk's retreat brought matters to a crisis. James wished to take advantage of Norfolk's evident discomfiture, to pursue him and bring him to battle, for the possibility of gaining a victory was obviously far greater than he had dared to hope. But his resolve to advance brought him face to face with the failure of his relations with his nobility. "It appears," wrote Tytler, ". . . to have been a rule amongst these feudal barons, which, if not strictly a part of the military law, had become established by custom, that they were not bound to act offensively within the territories of a foreign state, although their feudal tenure compelled them, under the penalty of forfeiture, to obey the royal command in repelling an enemy who had crossed the Borders and encamped within the Kingdom."[30]

When James ordered them to advance into England they refused to do so, as they had refused to follow Albany in 1523 and 1524. To some of them James doubtless appeared to be fighting a pointless war which was nothing more than a Border incident grown to national proportions; to others, those who favoured the Reformation, he doubtless appeared to be fighting as the champion of the Pope and the Catholic powers against a Protestant King. Not even Henry's claim to suzerainty seems to have aroused much anti-English feeling. Tempers ran high against those who were loyal to the King, who were termed "pensioners of the priests", and there was talk of a repetition of the affair of Lauder Bridge, when a group of lords led by the fifth Earl of Angus had refused to follow the King's grandfather James III to war, and had made him pay the penalty for slighting his lords by hanging six men to whom he had shown too much favour and turned for advice. At Fala Muir, however, the lords were less unanimous: "they could not agree among themselves about those who should stretch the ropes, everyone striving to save his kinsman or friend."[31] In the end there were no hangings; but neither was there an advance. The army disbanded, and the King, overwhelmed with humiliation, had no choice but to ride back to Edinburgh.

In the bitterness of that humiliation James "avouched publicly that the nobility neither loved his honour nor desired his continuance amongst them."; but he also declared his determination to see more military action against England "before the light of this moon ended". He was not wrong in sensing that Scotland possessed a military advantage, and in being determined not to waste it. He could still look for a certain amount of loyal support, for even if the majority of the lords had turned against him, he still had strong partisans in Cardinal Beaton, in his half-brother Moray, and in Lord Maxwell, the Warden of the Marches. For the reassurance of loyal friendship he turned to Oliver Sinclair. According to John Knox's narrative of the last months of the reign, it was after his humiliation at Fala Muir that James accepted from Sinclair, from the Laird of Ross, another man generally detested as a "minion" of the King, and from "utheris" who were strong supporters of Beaton, a "black list" containing the names of those lords and lairds who were suspected of heresy, and against whom proceedings could be taken when the King's position permitted. Considerable alarm was generated by the rumour that one of the names on the list was that of Arran. Whether or not the "black list" indeed existed, belief in its existence may have made the ultimate contribution to the poisoning of relations between the King and his lords. The King reputedly pocketed the "black list" for future attention and turned to his new military preparations.[32]

Two new forces were raised, one under Cardinal Beaton and the Earl of Moray, who marched to Haddington, as though intending to invade England on the east; the other, under the King and Lord Maxwell, was to invade England on the west. It finally numbered about 10,000 men. On reaching the west of Scotland, however, the King was either taken ill or collapsed with nervous strain. He retired to Lochmaben Castle to await the result of the invasion which took place without him. It was probably from Lochmaben that he wrote to Marie de Guise a strangely incoherent letter, in which he told her "I have received the letter which you were pleased to write to me, for which I thank you very humbly, assuring you that your man will not be oblige – " He was evidently incapable of continuing, for he resumed the letter with the words "I have been very ill these three days past, as I never was in my life."[33] No evidence survives of the nature of the King's illness, but his condition must have been very serious to keep him from an engagement which he had been so determined should take place.

The generally accepted account of what befell the invading force is principally derived from the narrative of John Knox, which is extremely vivid, but should not perhaps be accepted without question.

According to Knox, the Bishops of Scotland had been in charge of raising the force, and by them "letters were sent to such as they would charge to meet the King, day and place appointed." To Lochmaben came "companies from all quarters, as they were appointed, no man knowing

of any other . . . neither yet did the multitude know anything of the purpose till after midnight, when that the
trumpet blew and commanded all men to march forward,
and follow the King, (who was constantly supposed to have
been in the host.)"[34]

The invading force marched south through the night of
24th November, and in the morning encountered a force
under Sir Thomas Wharton near the Solway Moss, a
marshy area beside the River Esk. According to Knox,
and to all ensuing narratives, the King had decided that
Oliver Sinclair should command the force in his absence;
but it was only when battle was about to be joined that
the King's absence was revealed. Then, "thought Oliver
time to show his glory; and so incontinent (i.e. at once) was
displayed the King's banner; Oliver upon spears lift up
upon men's shoulders, and there with sound of trumpet
was he proclaimed general lieutenant . . . There was present
the Lord Maxwell, Warden, to whom the regiment, (i.e.
command) in absence of the King, properly appertained . . .
There was also present the Earls Glencairn and Cassillis,
with the Lord Fleming, and many other lords, barons and
gentlemen of Lothian, Fife, Angus and Mearns."[35] (Their
presence, incidentally, disposes of Knox's own previous description of an exclusively ecclesiastically-raised force.) Led
by Maxwell, they refused to submit to the command of
Sinclair; uproar broke out, and the force was reduced to
complete disorder, and was at Wharton's mercy.

Drummond, however, who though writing in the next
century evidently had access to contemporary sources
of information, gives a different version of the cause of
the trouble. "It hath been reported by those who were
acquainted with Oliver," he wrote, "that the commission
was not read, but that at his very sight such a tumult,
confused clamour, and inter-shouldering of malcontents
arose, their ranks were broken, the military order turned
into confusion, none so repining as the Lord Maxwell and

the Borderers, who, if he had patience to have heard the commission (as Oliver protested) was Lieutenant, and not he, whose charge was only to present it."[36]

James V has been much condemned for giving the command of the invading force to his favourite, who was obviously less well qualified for it than Lord Maxwell, and whom the lords could scarcely have been expected to obey willingly. It lends an extra dimension of tragedy to the disaster which ensued if the King's intention had been thus misconstrued and Maxwell indeed intended to have had the command.

The rout of Solway Moss was total. Without leadership "the soldiers cast from them their pikes, culverins and other weapons fensible; the horsemen left their spears; and so without judgment all men fled." There were few Scottish casualties, but many prisoners were taken although the English force was very much the smaller. Indeed, many of the prisoners, in the words of Knox "ran to houses and rendered themselves to women". Among the prisoners were all the lords previously named by Knox, and also Oliver Sinclair, whom he reported as taken "fleeing full manfully."

Sir Thomas Wharton, in his report of the engagement, numbered his own force at 300, but estimated the whole of the English force, including other parties which joined his own before the fighting began, at about 1,200. He made no mention of the Oliver Sinclair episode; possibly he was too far away to see what caused the trouble. He merely reported that the Scots advanced and then retired in disorder. He reported the taking of 1,200 prisoners and mentioned that only twenty Scots were slain though there were "divers drowned in the Esk".[37] Perhaps the most damning comment of all upon the failure of James V's relations with his nobility was that Scottish nobles were "not unwilling to become prisoners, rather than die in the service of a King in whom so many of his subjects had completely lost confidence."[38]

In the evening following the action the news of the defeat was brought to the King at Lochmaben. Ill as he was, lately the victim of personal misfortune, and more recently the victim of the terrible humiliation to himself and his sovereignty offered at Fala Muir, James had no resilience to withstand the impact of the news. He had been utterly unprepared to receive it, and upon receiving it he "was stricken with a sudden fear and astonishment, so that scarcely could he speak, or hold purpose with any man. The night constrained him to remain where he was, and so (he) went to bed; but rose without rest or quiet sleep. His continual complaint was 'Oh, fled Oliver? Is Oliver tane? Oh fled Oliver?' And these words in his melancholy, and as it were carried away in a trance, repeated he from time to time, to the very hour of his death."[39] Apparently the aspect of the defeat which preyed most upon his mind was the failure of even his favourite, his trusted friend, to show personal bravery on his behalf. Whether Oliver Sinclair could have been expected to stand alone when others fled is another matter.

The defeat of Solway Moss was indeed a disaster beyond exaggeration for the King. For this there were two reasons. Firstly, the army which had marched to Fala Muir had been the national muster of Scotland; its refusal to march into England left the King without his principal military resource. Secondly, the force which the King had intended to lead into England had been in a sense a private army, in that it had been raised by "privy letters" not by a general muster. With his second army defeated James had no further military resources upon which to draw; he had lost the military advantage which he had temporarily possessed when his army was encamped on Fala Muir. James cannot have doubted that Henry VIII would gather his strength, invade Scotland, and assert his claim to suzerainty with overwhelming force. It would be merely a matter of time, and that not long. Without a major battle James V had been utterly defeated; and unlike his father he had had the misfortune to survive.

Whatever the future held for the King of Scots he could see in it nothing but some kind of disgrace for himself, and for his country reduction to the status of a province of England. It was little wonder that he surrendered to despair. He left Lochmaben and rode back to Edinburgh, where he met Cardinal Beaton, who at the news of the defeat of the King's force had retired from Haddington. According to Knox they were almost ashamed to look each other in the face, both having set out so determinedly, neither having achieved anything. Both faced a future threatened by the shadow of English domination; but with future affairs the King had no further concern. He had not recovered from the illness to which he had succumbed at Lochmaben; increasingly ill, and uncaring, he left Edinburgh and rode purposelessly from place to place.

Knox has much to say of the King's last days, and from his narrative derive the anecdotes which have been frequently retold of them. From Edinburgh the King rode to Tantallon, where, according to an English report sent to Henry VIII, he had "a mistress in the keeping of Oliver Sinclair's wife."[40] Thence he rode to Linlithgow to visit the Queen who was in the last month of her third pregnancy. He did not long remain with her, but continued his purposeless journeying. He came to Hallyards, in Fife, the seat of his Treasurer, Sir William Kirkcaldy of Grange. He was received by the Lady of Grange, who gave him support, and "began to comfort him" and willed him to take the work of God in good part. 'My portion (said he) of this world is short, for I will not be with you fifteen days.' " Knox, who records this incident, describes how he referred continually to his approaching death. "His servants repairing to him, asked where he would have provision made for his Yule? (i.e. where he intended to spend Christmas) ... He answered, with a disdainful smirk, 'I cannot tell; choose ye the place, but this I can tell you, 'ere Yule day, ye will be masterless, and the realm without a King.'"

It was the beginning of December when he came to Falkland, and there, overcome with the spiritual fatigue of despair, he took to his bed. "And albeit there appeared unto him no signs of death, yet he constantly affirmed, before such a day, 'I shall be dead'." On 7th December at Linlithgow, Marie de Guise bore her third child, the daughter who was destined to become Mary, Queen of Scots. The story of how the King received the news of her birth is well known, in the version of Pitscottie. When the messenger told him that the Queen had borne him a fair daughter, he replied – referring to the fact that the Crown had come to the House of Stewart through the marriage of Margery, daughter of Robert the Bruce, to Walter the High Steward – "Adieu, Farewell, it came with a lass, it will pass with a lass." He had no hope for himself, but if the Queen had borne a son he might have died with some hope for the future of his dynasty. James III had died at the hands of his own subjects; yet his subjects had rallied to support his son. But the hope that the lords who had repudiated him would defend his kingdom for the sake of his son was denied to James V: the birth of a daughter seemed to place the fate of Scotland irrevocably in the hands of Henry VIII. Drummond, in his account of the King's death, makes James voice this thought: "The Crown came by a woman, and it will with one go; many miseries approach this poor kingdom; King Henry will either take it by his arms or marriage."

James survived the infliction of this ultimate despair by one week, during which time he spoke little, but lay awaiting death, his face turned to the wall. Death came on 14th December, while the King's bed was surrounded by a company which included Cardinal Beaton, the Earls of Argyll and Rothes, Sir William Kirkcaldy and Sir David Lindsay of the Mount. The King "turned him back" and saw them, and then "gave a little smile and laughter", kissed his hand to them, "and thereafter held up his hands to God and yielded the spirit."[42] The life which so ended had not been long; James V had lived thirty years, eight months and four days.

It was recounted by John Major that people would often compare the Kings of the House of Stewart to the horses of the district of Mar, "which in youth are good but in their old age bad." In fact, since the reigns of the earliest Stewart Kings, Robert II and Robert III, far beyond the memory of sixteenth century people, no King had lived to reach old age. In that tragic series of Kings, all of whom had died by violence in youth or early middle age, the last years of each one had been years not so much of deterioration as of infinite fatigue. In the case of James I, captivity in England had taken the place of a minority in Scotland. But the four succeeding Kings had all endured more exhausting and demanding experiences by the time they reached the end of adolescence than most men endure in the course of a long lifetime. And each of them had faced in his later years the knowledge of one or other variety of failure, the most wearying of all forms of self-knowledge. For James V the conviction that his failure would be followed by the extinction of his dynasty was the *coup de grâce*.

CONCLUSION

"All is lost"

James V

As early as 1537 the Duke of Norfolk had been able to write of James V "So sore a dread King and so ill-beloved of his subjects was never in this land." But the subjects to whom Norfolk referred were the lords of Scotland, James died still popular with the common people.

Various amiable aspects of his popular image lived on in the public mind. Insubstantial and yet attractive was the picture of him which inspired the two folk poems "The Gaberlunzie Man" and "The Jolly Beggar" – the picture of the King as an adventurous and insouciant amorist. His long series of mistresses and his casual sexual adventures have always been regarded as proof that he was a highly successful lover. But possibly the implication is rather that he was an isolated man on the whole unsuccessful in forming close and lasting relationships. Most of his affairs were brief, and although he experienced a strong enough passion for Margaret Erskine to be prepared at one time to throw aside every consideration of diplomatic and financial advantage in order to marry her, the fact remains that he did not do so. Considerations of orthodoxy, foreign policy and financial necessity won the day against passion. Furthermore, neither of his marriages was a love-match. In the persons of Madeleine and Marie de Guise James V wedded France. The fact that he had a mistress in the last months of the reign naturally gave rise to the supposition that he did not greatly love his second Queen. He seems to have respected her, as she deserved; but with this relationship, as with most others, the overall impression is that he was not very deeply involved.

Throughout his reign James had shown himself concerned with the administration of effective justice, not indeed for love of justice as an ideal, but as a means of imposing law and order. The belief that James V was "a good and sure justiciar" even survived his execution of three people who were generally believed innocent: the Master of Forbes, Sir James Hamilton of Finnart and Lady Glamis. The reason for this was possibly that both the Master of Forbes and Hamilton of Finnart were so unpopular and so widely regarded as wicked that their supposed innocence of the crimes for which they died, only temporarily made their executions seem scandalous. In the case of Lady Glamis, though her fate aroused public pity at the time, the fact that she died by burning, the common fate of witches, led gradually to the growth of the belief that she had been burnt for witchcraft – an error which is still repeated. General belief in the scrupulosity of the King's justice was therefore scarcely impaired by these executions.

More surprising was the survival of the King's popular image, the "King of the Commons" and the "Gudeman of Ballengiech", in the face of his support of the Catholic Church which had lost its hold over the common people, of his support of the Catholic clergy who had won themselves popular contempt, and of his connection with the Church's persecution of the Reformers. The answer perhaps is that the King was regarded rather as the victim of his advisers, "his papist bishops", than as their supporter. The passage of time would surely have eroded this belief. If the story of the "black list" were true, it suggests that the King would have persecuted in the future with greater enthusiasm. The spread of Lutheran or subsequently of Calvinist ideas to that class with which his relations were already bad would inevitably have hardened his attitude.

Therefore it seems that the survival of the most amiable aspect of his image was largely due to his early death, which took place before the spread of the Reformation drove him to act with the severity shown by other Catholic sovereigns in the ensuing decades.

The unpopularity which James would surely have won had he lived longer, and continued to adhere to the policy which he had followed throughout his reign, was the unhappy heritage of Marie de Guise, who was personally a Catholic of strong conviction and did not doubt that her political duty was to hand on a Catholic kingdom to her daughter.

Marie de Guise, however, did not become head of state upon the death of her husband, as Margaret Tudor had done. Margaret may have offered a discouraging example of the troubles which could be caused by a woman in power, or Marie herself may have been too closely identified with the unpopular policy of James V. At all events, there was a struggle for the regency which provided a macabre epilogue to the reign. According to Scottish custom, and according to the most recent precedent, the proper regent for Mary Queen of Scots was her nearest adult male kinsman, the Earl of Arran. Marie de Guise's opinion of Arran was succinctly expressed; to her he was "the most inconstant man in the world." It has always been assumed that resistance against the appointment of Arran was planned by Marie de Guise and Cardinal Beaton, and that when Beaton produced a paper which he claimed was the will of James V, which named himself, the King's half-brother Moray and the Earls of Huntly and Argyll as co-regents, the paper was a forgery. Arran accused Beaton of having taken the dying King's hand and forcibly used it to subscribe a blank paper. Knox followed him in reporting "Many affirm a dead man's hand was made to subscribe a blank". The accusation received general acceptance, Arran became regent, and Beaton was temporarily imprisoned.

The accusation made by Arran was proved untrue in 1886 when the "will" was discovered among the Hamilton Papers. No signature purporting to be that of James V was on it. Technically it was not a will but a "notarial instrument" – a means under Scots law of preserving evidence – signed by eleven witnesses. The signatures included those of Sir William Kirkcaldy of Grange, James V's Treasurer, Sir James Learmont, his Master of the Household, and John Tennant, one of his most trusted personal servants. There is no reason to doubt that the notarial instrument embodied the genuine wishes of James V.[1] Beaton had been defeated not by the unmasking of a forgery but by his own unpopularity and the unpopularity of the Church which he represented. It may be added that to have forced the dying King to sign a blank piece of paper would have been impossible, considering how many people were present at his death bed.

Arran, established as regent, in July 1543 negotiated with Henry VIII the Treaties of Greenwich, a peace treaty between Scotland and England and a marriage treaty between the infant Queen of Scots and Henry's heir, Prince Edward. It was further agreed that the Queen of Scots should be sent to live at the English Court. Arran was rewarded with a promise of the hand of Henry's daughter Elizabeth for his son. Cardinal Beaton, however, on securing his freedom in September, quickly achieved a personal ascendancy over Arran, and in December he caused the Treaties of Greenwich to be repudiated. His action led to the English invasions of 1544 and 1545 in which Henry showed his resentment by a devastation of the Borders, which the Scots named "The Rough Wooing". Henry died in 1547, and the Earl of Hertford, who had led the invasions, became Duke of Somerset and regent for Edward VI. He continued Henry's policy by invading Scotland in 1547, when he won the battle of Pinkie Cleugh, which caused the Scots severe losses but achieved nothing politically. As had happened in the past, English military resources proved great enough to inflict defeat upon the Scots, but not great enough to impose English domination. The danger that Scotland would become an English province in the reign of Edward VI was finally frustrated by Marie de Guise who in 1548 sent her daughter to be brought up at the Court of France.

In May 1546 Cardinal Beaton had been murdered at St Andrews; but Marie de Guise, in spite of the loss of her strongest ally, gained greatly in strength through the military support she received from France. She strengthened the ties between France and Scotland by a visit to France in 1550, which paved the way for her taking over the regency from Arran. Marie became regent in 1554 and Arran was compensated for his loss of office with the French duchy of Châtelhérault. When Mary Queen of Scots reached the age of sixteen in 1558 she was married to the Dauphin François, the eldest son of Henri II and Catherine de Medici. Then, the following year, upon the death of Henri, the Dauphin became François II of France. Queen Mary, however, did not long remain both sovereign of Scotland and Queen consort of France; in 1560 François died, leaving Mary a widow at the age of eighteen. The death of Marie de Guise in the same year left Mary no choice but to return and rule her native kingdom.

Marie de Guise, confident that her daughter would be brought up as a Catholic Queen, had endeavoured to conserve for her a Catholic kingdom. But Scotland had turned predominantly Protestant in sentiment under Marie's Catholic regency, and the help given by Elizabeth I of England to the Protestant Lords of the Congregation, who led the Reformation Rebellion in Scotland, ensured that Mary, Queen of Scots would return as a Catholic sovereign to rule a Protestant country.

Mary was very much the daughter of James V. Like him she was very royal in her generosity to her poorer subjects and her desire to give them a parental protection. Like him she was never on easy terms with her nobility. Like him she was a convinced Catholic, yet by nature, not a persecutor. But Mary was even less fortunate than her father. In his reign the Reformation had been a threatening cloud, in hers it was an engulfing storm, and she was no more equipped to come to terms with it than he had been. The failure of the spiritual authority and the political power of the Catholic Church in Scotland during the reign of Mary was the logical conclusion of the events of the previous reign.

It was no small part of Mary's tragedy that "she came from the old, lax Catholic World",[2] the world of James V; and it was not the Crown, as James V had feared, but the Catholic Scotland he had known that "passed with a lass."

Notes and References

Chapter One: KING AND COUNTRY

1. Pitscottie, *Historie and Cronicles of Scotland* Vol. I, p. 408.
2. Drummond, *History of Scotland*, pp. 348-9
3. Hume-Brown, *History of Scotland.* Vol. 1, p. 396.
4. Donaldson, *Scotland, James V to James VII*, p. 62.
5. Knox, *History of The Reformation in Scotland*, Vol. I, pp. 92-3.
6. Dickinson, Donaldson and Milne, *A Source-book of Scottish History.* Vol. II, pp. 9-10.
7. Ibid., p. 10.
8. Ibid., p. 8.
9. Donaldson, op. cit., p. 5.
10. Mackie, *A History of Scotland*, p. 102.
11. Barbour, The Brus, cit. Wallace Notestein, *The Scot in History*, p. 33.

Chapter Two: THE KING'S MINORITY

1. Mackie, *Henry VIII and Scotland*, Transactions of the Royal Historical Society, 4th Series, Vol. XXIX, p. 102.
2. August 26th, 1514. *Acts of the Lords of Council in Public Affairs*, p. 19.
3. Dacre to English Privy Council, 4th August 1515. *Letters and Papers . . of Henry VIII*, Vol. II, pt. I, No. 783.
4. *Letters and Papers . . . of Henry VIII*, Vol. II, pt. I, p. clxxxi.
5. The Cartel of La Bastie, *cit.* Marie W. Stuart, *The Scot who was a Frenchman*, p. 17.
6. Ibid., Appendix E, p. 300.
7. In spite of the bitterness of Margaret's complaints, Angus had, from his own viewpoint, some reason for claiming Ettrick Forest as his: Robert the Bruce had granted it to his faithful

supporter "The Good Lord James" Douglas, though the Douglas family had subsequently forfeited it. Ettrick Forest became a royal forest, used for hunting until James V turned it over to sheep. Infra. p. xxx.

8. Scarisbrick, *Henry VIII*, p. 126.
9. *Acts of the Lords of Council in Public Affairs*, pp. 180-1.
10. The details of the siege of Wark and of the winter weather come from George Buchanan's *History of Scotland*, pp. 149-150. Buchanan had the only military experience of his life as a very young volunteer on this expedition.

Chapter Three: THE ASCENDANCY OF ANGUS.

1. *Letters and Papers . . . of Henry VIII*, Vol. III., No. 1890.
2. Further information on sixteenth century materials etc. can be found in *Handbook of English Costume in the Sixteenth Century* by C. W. and P. Cunnington (London, 1954).
3. The Dream of Sir David Lindsay *Works* Vol. I, p. 4.
4. The Complaint of Sir David Lindsay. *Works*. Vol. I, p. 42.
5. The Dream of Sir David Lindsay. *Works*. Vol. I, p. 5.
6. Farmer, *A History of Music in Scotland*, p. 76.
7. *State Papers of Henry VIII*, Vol. IV, No. xciii.
8. Chapman, *The Sisters of Henry VIII*, p. 81.
9. *State Papers of Henry VIII*, Vol. IV, p. 198.
10. Drummond, *History of Scotland*, p. 282.
11. Ibid., p. 285.
12. Buchanan, *History of Scotland*, p. 155.
13. *Accounts of the Lord High Treasurer*, Vol. V pp. 275, 306.
14. Ibid., p. 416.
15. The Complaint of Sir David Lindsay, *Works*, Vol. I, p. 46.
16. Ibid.
17. Lindsay, *Works*. Vol. IV, Introduction, p. xlii.
18. For a discussion of the matter, see *Exchequer Rolls*, Vol. XV, Preface, pp. li-lv.
19. Donaldson, *Scotland, James V to James VII*, p. 41.

Chapter Four: KING OF SCOTS.

1. Stuart, *The Scot who was a Frenchman*, p. 254.

2. J. Huizinga, *The Waning of the Middle Ages*. (Peregrine, reprint 1968) p. 52.
3. Dickinson, Donaldson and Milne, *A Sourcebook of Scottish History*, Vol. II, p. 28.
4. Buchanan, *History of Scotland*, p. 162.
5. Dickinson, Donaldson and Milne, *op. cit.* Vol. II, pp. 29-31.
6. James V to Henry VIII, Jedburgh, 23rd July, 1529. cit. Tytler, *History of Scotland*, Vol. V, p. 192.
7. B.M. MSS. Calig. B. ii. 224. Cit. Tytler. *op. cit.* Vol. V, p. 192.
8. Ibid.
9. Robertson, *An Introduction to the Poetry of Scotland* . . . p. 357.
10. Pitcairn, *Ancient Criminal Trials in Scotland*, Vol. I, pt. I, p. 154.
11. Donaldson, *Scotland James V to James VII*, p. 50.
12. *Acts of the Lords of Council in Public Affairs*, pp. 356-8.
13. Northumberland to Henry VIII, 27th December, 1531. *cit.* Tytler, *op. cit.* Vol. V, p. 200. As far as Crawford was concerned, the King had apparently taken from him certain lands which he possessed in the Isles, and had given them to Maclain of Ardnamurchan, "which hath engendered a great hatred in the said Earl's heart against the said Scots King." Ibid., p. 201.
14. Ibid., p. 200.
15. Pitscottie, *Historie and Cronicles of Scotland*, Vol. I, pp. 335-8.
16. Buchanan, *op. cit.*, p. 181.
17. Robertson, *op. cit.*, p. 356.
18. Ibid., p. 179.
19. The Answer which Sir David Lindsay made to the King's Flyting. *Works*, Vol. I, p. 104.

Chapter Five: THE ANCIENT ALLIANCE AND THE OLD RELIGION — I.

1. Donaldson, *Scotland, James V to James VII*, p. 43.
2. *Letters and Papers . . . of Henry VIII*, Vol. III, No. 5531. See also, *Letters of James V*, p. 152.
3. Donaldson, *op. cit.*, p. 46.
4. Hannay, *The College of Justice* . . ., p. 33.
5. *Acts of the Lords of Council* . . . Introd. p. xxxviii.
6. Hannay, *op. cit.*, p. 35.
7. Tytler, *History of Scotland*, Vol. V, p. 208.

8. *State Papers of Henry VIII*, Vol. IX, p. 172.

9. Donaldson, *Scotland, James V to James VII*, p. 47.

10. Knox, *History of the Reformation in Scotland*, Vol. I, p. 60.

11. Maclean, *A Concise History of Scotland*, p. 94

12 *Letters of James V*, p. 295.

13. *Letters and Papers . . . of Henry VIII*, Vol. X, No. 862.

14. Ibid., No. 1069.

15. Drummond, *History of Scotland*, p. 310.

16. Knox, *History of the Reformation in Scotland*, Vol. I, pp. 72-5.

17. Most of the available information on Duthie and his shrine is collected in the essay "Loretto" in *In Byways of Scottish History* by Louis A. Barbé.

18. *Letters of James V*, p. 235.

19. Donaldson, *op. cit.*, p. 60.

20. Pitscottie, *Historie and Cronicles of Scotland*, Vol. I, pp. 362-3.

21. Ibid.

22. Brantôme, *Book of the Ladies: Illustrious Dames*, p. 224.

23. Anon. *Elegie Nuptiale . . .*

24. Pitscottie, *op. cit.* Vol. I, p. 365.

25. Lévis Mirepoix *et al.*, François 1er, pp. 216-17.

26. Gardiner and Wallop to Lord Lisle, Blois, 21st November, 1536. *Letters and Papers . . . of Henry VIII*, Vol. XI, No. 1130.

27. Registres due Parlement, 1536. Du dimanche, dernier jour de décembre, l'an 1536. cit. Tevlet, *Papiers d'État . . .* Vol. I, p. 124.

28. *Letters and Papers . . . of Henry VIII*, Vol. XI, No. 916. i.

29. Ibid., No. 916 i and ii.

30. Pitscottie, *op. cit.* Vol. I, p. 369.

31. The Deploratioun of the Deith of Quene Magdalene, Lindsay, *Works*, Vol. I, pp. 106-12.

Chapter Six: THE ANCIENT ALLIANCE AND THE
OLD RELIGION — II.

1. Deploration sur le trepas de très noble Princesse Madame Magdalaine de France . . . *see* Lindsay, *Works*. Vol. III, pp. 129-30.

2. Bapst, *Les Mariages de Jacques V*, p. 316.

3. Ibid., p. 320.

4. Ibid., p. 321.

5. Mitchison, *A History of Scotland*, p. 98.
6. Pitcairn, *Ancient Criminal Trials in Scotland*, Vol. I, pt. I, p. 84.
7. Tytler, *History of Scotland*, Vol. V, p. 219.
8. Pitcairn, *op. cit.*, Vol. I, pt. I, p. 189.
9. Tytler, *op. cit.*, Vol. V. Proofs and illustrations, *The Conspiracy of Lady Glamis*, p. 369.
10. Ibid., p. 370. On this occasion twenty-eight members of the jury were fined for non-appearance. But "a refusal of this kind was in fact a proof of the power, not of the innocence, of the party accused." Ibid., p. 373.
11. Hume of Godscroft, *cit.* Pitcairn, *op. cit.*, Vol. I, pt. I, p. 195.
12. Pitscottie, *Historie and Cronicles of Scotland*, Vol. I, pp. 378-80.
13. Dickinson, Donaldson and Milne, *A Sourcebook of Scottish History*, Vol. II, pp. 99-105.
14. A portion of *Franciscanus*, paraphrased by P. Hume Brown in *George Buchanan . . .* p. 95.
15. Robertson, *An Introduction to the Poetry of Scotland . . .*, p. 220.
16. Lindsay, *Works*, Vol. II, p. 38.
17. Ibid, p. 108.
18. Sir William Eure to Thomas Cromwell, 26th January 1540. B. M. MSS. Reg. 7. C. xvi fol. 136-9. *See* Lindsay. *Works*, Vol. II, pp. 2-4.
19. *State Papers and Letters of Sir Ralph Sadler*, Vol. I, pp. 17-45.
20. *Letters of James V*, p. 377.
21. Pinkerton, *The History of Scotland . . .* Vol. II, p. 361.

Chapter Seven: VAIN GLORY

1. Lesley, *History of Scotland*, p. 167.
2. *Letters of James V*, p. 399.
3. Tytler, *History of Scotland*, Vol. V, p. 231.
4. Donaldson, *Scotland, James V to James VII*, p. 53. "Lord Gray was owing 10,000 merks and did not pay the balance of 7,000 until 1543" – after the King's death – "Colquhoun of Luss owed £1,000 and paid the final instalment in 1546."
5. Stewart, *The Scottish Coinage*, p. 78.
6. Donaldson, *op. cit.*, p. 58.
7. Farmer, *A History of Music in Scotland*, pp. 77, 92, 93.
8. *Accounts of the Masters of Works . . .* Vol. I, p. xiii.

9. *Registrum Secreti Sigilli, cit. Accounts of Masters of Works*, Vol. I, p. Lviii.
10. Ibid. xxxiii-iv.
11. Cruden, *The Scottish Castle*, p. 148.
12. Moncrieffe of that Ilk, *Falkland Palace*, pp. 4, 19.
13. Cruden, *op. cit.*, pp. 146-7.
14. Richardson and Beveridge. *Linlithgow Palace*, p. 10.
15. Richardson, *The Abbey and Palace of Holyroodhouse*, p. 5.
16. Cruden, *op. cit.*, p. 145.
17. *Accounts of the Masters of Works* . . . Vol. I, p. xiii.
18. Moncrieffe of that Ilk, *op. cit.*, p. 145.
19. Richardson and Beveridge. *op. cit.* pp. 16-17.
20. Strickland, *The Queens of Scotland*, Vol. I, p. 380.
21. Drummond, *History of Scotland*, pp. 333-5.
22. H.M.C. 3rd Rep. p. 393. *cit. D.N.B.*, Vol. VIII, p. 1051.
23. *State Papers of Henry VIII*, Vol. V, p. 160.
24. Donaldson, *op. cit.*, p. 53.
25. Tytler, *op. cit.*, Vol. V, p. 241.
26. Ibid., p. 242.
27. Ibid., p. 243. The Archbishop's findings were incorporated into Henry's claim to suzerainty over Scotland, which he made on 5th November, 1542.
28. *Letters and Papers* . . . *of Henry VIII*, Vol. XVII, No. 1033.
29. Ibid., No. 1060. Cardinal Beaton seconded the King with a letter to the same effect. Ibid., No. 1072.
30. Tytler, *op. cit.*, Vol. V. p. 247.
31. Drummond, *op. cit.*, p. 339.
32. Knox, *History of the Reformation in Scotland*, Vol. I, p. 84.
33. Strickland, *op. cit.*, Vol. I, p. 402.
34. Knox, *op. cit.*, Vol. I, p. 84-5.
35. Ibid., p. 86.
36. Drummond, *op. cit.*, p. 343.
37. *Letters and Papers* . . . *of Henry VIII*, Vol. XVII, No. 1142.
38. Donaldson, *op. cit.*, p. 60.
39. Knox, *op. cit.*, Vol. I, pp. 89-90.
40. *Letters and Papers* . . . *of Henry VIII*, Vol. XVII, No. 1194. Lord Lisle to Henry VIII, 12th December, 1542.
41. Knox, *op. cit.*, Vol. I, p. 91.
42. Pitscottie, *Historie and Cronicles of Scotland*, Vol. I, pp. 407-8.

Conclusion.

1. Masson, *Scotland the Nation*, pp. 374-7.
2. David Mathew, *James I.* p. 16.

Appendix A

FULL TEXT OF THE BALLAD *Johnie Armstrong*, IN ORIGINAL
SPELLING.

In the ballad version of Gilnockie's fate the King writes him
a "luving letter", summoning Gilnockie to "cum and speik
with him". The subsequent execution takes on a worse
appearance from the fact that Gilnockie approached the
King under safe conduct.

Pitcairn's *Ancient Criminal Trials in Scotland* gives the
name of Gilnockie's brother, the Laird of Mangertoun, as
Thomas. In the ballad Gilnockie addresses him as "Kirsty,
my brother," and bids him farewell unaware that he also
is about to meet his death.

Johnie Armstrong.

Sum speiks of lords, sum speiks of lairds,
And sic lyke men of hie degrie;
Of a gentleman I sing a sang,
Sum tyme called Laird of Gilnockie.

The King he wrytes a luving letter,
With his ain hand sae tenderly,
And he hath sent it to Johnie Armstrong,
To cum and speik with him speedily.

The Eliots and Armstrongs did convene;
They were a gallant cumpanie –
"We'll ride and meit our lawful King,
And bring him safe to Gilnockie."

'Make kinnen and capon ready, then,
And venison in great plentie;
We'll wellcum here our royal King;
I hope he'll dine at Gilnockie!' –

They ran their horses on the Langholme howm,
And brak their spears wi' mickle main;
The ladies lukit frae their loft windows –
'God bring our men weel hame agen!'

When Johnie cam' before the King,
Wi' a' his men sae brave to see,
The King he movit his bonnet to him:
He ween'd he was King as well as he.

'May I find grace, my sovereign liege,
Grace for my loyal men and me?
For my name it is Johnie Armstrong,
And a subject of yours, my liege,' said he.

'Away, away, thou traitor strang!
Out o' my sight soon maust thou be!
I grantit never a traitor's life,
And now I'll not begin wi' thee.' –

'Grant me my life, my liege, my King!
And a bonny gift I'll gie to thee:
Full four-and-twenty milk-white steids,
Were a' foal'd in ae year to me.

'I'll gie thee a' these milk-white steids,
That prance and nicker at a speir;
And as mickle gude Inglish gilt,
As four o' their braid backs dow bear' –

'Away, away, thou traitor strang!
Out o' my sight soon mayst thou be!
I grantit never a traitor's life,
And now I'll not begin wi' thee!' –

'Grant me my life, my liege, my King!
And a bonny gift I'll gie to thee:
Gude four-and-twenty ganging mills,
That gang thro a' the year to me.

'These four-and-twenty mills complete
Sall gang for thee thro' a' the yeir;
And as mickle of gude reid wheit,
As a' thair happers dow to bear.' –

'Away, away, thou traitor strang!
Out o' my sight soon mayst thou be!
I grantit never a traitor's life,
And now I'll not begin wi' thee.' –

'Grant me my life, ly liege, my King!
And a great, great gift I'll gie to thee;
Bauld four-and-twenty sisters' sons,
Sall for thee fecht, tho' a' should flee!' –

'Away, away, thou traitor strang!
Out o' my sight soon mayst thou be!
I grantit never a traitor's life,
And now I'll not begin wi' thee.' –

'Grant me my life, my liege, my King!
And a brave gift I'll gie to thee:
All between heir and Newcastle town
Sall pay their yeirly rent to thee.' –

'Away, away, thou traitor strang!
Out o' my sight soon mayst thou be!
I grantit never a traitor's life,
And now I'll not begin wi' thee' –

'Ye lied, ye lied, now, King,' he says,
'Altho' a King and Prince ye be!
For I've luved naething in my life,
I weel dare say it, but honesty:

'Save a fat horse, and a fair woman,
Twa bonny dogs to kill a deir;
But England suld have found me meal and mault,
Gif I had lived this hundred yeir!

'She suld have found me meal and mault,
And beef and mutton in a' plentie;
But never a Scots wyfe could have said
That e'er I skaith'd her a puir flee.

'To seik het water beneath cauld ice,
Surely it is a griet folie –
I have asked grace at a graceless face;
But there is nane for my men and me!

'But had I kenn'd ere I cam' frae hame,
How thou unkind wadst been to me,
I wad have keepit the Border side;
In spite of all thy force and thee.

'Wist England's King that I was ta'en,
O gin a blythe man he wad be!
For anes I slew his sister's son,
And on his briest bane brak a trie!

John wore a girdle about his middle.
Imbroider'd owre wi' burning gold,
Bespangled wi' the same metal,
Maist beautiful was to behold.

There hung nine targats at Johnie's hat,
And ilk ane worth three hundred pound –
'What wants that knave that a King suld have,
But the sword of honour and the crown?

'O where got thou these targats, Johnie,
That blink sae brawlie abune thy brie?'
'I gat them in the field fechting,
Where, cruel King, thou durst not be.

'Had I my horse, and harness gude,
And riding as I ownt to be,
It suld have been tauld this hundred yeir,
The meeting of my King and me!

'God be with thee, Kirsty, my brother,
Lang live thou Laird of Mangertoun!
Lang mayst thou live on the Border syde,
Ere thou see thy brother ride up and doun!

'And God be with thee, Kirsty, my son,
Where thou sits on thy nurse's knee!
But an thou live this hundred yeir,
Thy father's better thou'lt never be.

'Farewell! my bonny Gilnock hall,
Where on Esk side thou standest stout:
Gif I had lived but seven yeirs mair,
I wad hae gilt thee round about.'

John was murdered at Carlinrigg.
And all his gallant companie;
But Scotland's heart was ne'er sae wae
To see sae mony brave men die –

Because they save their country deir
Frae Englishmen! Nane were sa bauld,
Whyle Johnie lived on the Border syde
Nane of them durst cum neir his hauld.

Appendix B

The Copy of the Notes of the Interlude.

"In the first entrance came in *Solace*, whose part was but to make merry, sing ballads with his fellows and drink at the interludes of the play, who showed first to all the audience the play to be played, which was a general thing meaning nothing in special to displease no man, praying therefore no man to be angry with the same.

Next came in a King, who passed to his throne, having no speech to the end of the play, and then to ratify and approve as in plain parliament all things done by the rest of the players, which represented the Three Estates. With him came his courtiers, *Placebo*, *Pickthank* and *Flattery*, and such a like guard, one swearing he was the lustiest, starkest, best proportioned and most valiant man that ever was, another swearing he was the best with long-bow, cross-bow and culverin in the world; Another swearing he was the best jouster and man of arms in the world, and so forth during their parts. Thereafter came a man armed in Marness with a sword drawn in his hand, a *Bishop*, a *Burgess*-man, and *Experience* clad like a doctor, who sat them all down on the dais, under the King.

After them came a *Poor Man*, who did go up and down the scaffold, making a heavy complaint, that he was harried through the courtiers taking his fen in one place and also his tacks in another place, wherethrough no had strayed his house, his wife and children begging their bread, and so of many thousand in Scotland, which would make the King's grace lose of men if his grace stood need, saying there was no remedy to be gotten, for though he would sue to the King's grace he was neither acquainted with Comptroller nor Treasurer, and without them might no man get no goodness of the King. After that he spread (i.e., asked) for the King. And when he was shown to the man that was *King* in the play he answered that he was no king, for there is but one king which made all and governeth all, who is Eternal, to whom he and all earthly kings are but officers, of the which they must make reckoning, and so forth, much more to that effect. And then he looked to the *King* and said he was not the King of Scotland, for there was another King in Scotland, that hanged John Armstrong with his fellows, and Sym the laird and many other more, which had pacified the country, and stanched theft; but he had left one thing undone, which pertained as well to his charge as the other.

And when he was asked what that was he made a long narration of the oppression of the poor, by taking of the corpse present beasts, and of the harrying of poor men by consistory law, and of many other abusions of the spiritualisty and Church, with many long stories and authorities. And then the *Bishop* rose and rebuked him saying it affaired not to him to speak such matters, commanding him silence, or else to suffer death for it by their law. Thereafter rose the man of arms, alleging the contrary, and commanded the poor man to speak, saying their abusion had been over long suffered without any law. Then the poor man showed the great abusion of Bishops, Prelates, Abbots, reiving men's wives and daughters and holding them, and of the maintaining of their children; and of their over-buying of lords, and barons, Eldest Sons to their daughters, wherethrough the nobility of the blood of the realm was degenerate; and of the great superfluous rents that pertained to the Church, by reason of over much temporal land given to them, which they proved that the King might take both by the Canon law and civil law; and of the great abominable vices that reign in cloisters, and of the common bordels that was kept in cloisters of nuns. All this was proved by *Experience*, and also was showed the office of a Bishop, and produced the New Testament, with the authorities to that effect.

And then rose the *Man of Arms* and the *Burgess*, and did say that all that was produced by the *Poor Man* and *Experience* was reasonable of verity, and of great effect, and very expedient to be reformed with the consent of parliament. And the *Bishop* said he would not consent thereunto. The *Man of Arms* and *Burgess* said they were two and he but one, wherefore their voice should have most effect. Thereafter the *King* in the play ratified, approved and confirmed all that was rehearsed."

*   *   *

This *Copy of the Notes of the Interlude* was sent by Sir William Eure to Thomas Cromwell, Lord Privy Seal of England. His covering letter contains the account of James V's reaction to the performance (see p. 154). The letter, written from Berwick on 26th January 1540, and the enclosure, are in the British Museum: MSS. Reg. 7. C. XVI. fols 136-139. They are reprinted in the Works of Sir David Lindsay ed Douglas Hamer, Vol II pp 2-6. In this Appendix the *Copy of the Notes* has been repunctuated and the spelling modernized.

Bibliography

I. RECORD SOURCES AND COLLECTIONS OF CORRESPONDENCE

Accounts of the Lord High Treasurer of Scotland 1473–1566. Ed. Thomas Dickson and Sir James Balfour Paul. (11 Vols. 1877–1916).

Accounts of the Masters of Works for building and repairing Royal Palaces and Castles. Vol. I. 1529–1615. Ed. Henry M. Paton. (Edinburgh, 1957).

Acts of the Lords of Council in Public Affairs, 1501–1544. Ed. Robert Kerr Hannay (1932).

Ancient Criminal Trials in Scotland. Ed. Robert Pitcairn. (3 Vols. Bannatyne and Maitland Clubs, 1829–1833).

Exchequer Rolls of Scotland, 1264–1600. (Various Editors. 23 Vols. 1878–1908.)

The Letters of King Henry VIII: a Selection, with a few other Documents. Ed. M. St Clare Byrne (London, 1936).

Letters and Papers, Foreign and Domestic of the Reign of Henry VIII, 1509–1547. Ed. Brewer, Gairdner and Brodie, (21 Vols. 1862–1910).

Letters of James V. Ed. Denys Hay. (1954).

Papiers d'Etat . . . relatifs à l'histoire de l'Ecosse au XVIᵉ Siècle. Ed. A. Teulet. (3 Vols. Bannatyne Club, 1852–1860.)

State Papers of Henry VIII. (11 Vols. 1830–1852).

State Papers and Letters of Sir Ralph Sadler. Ed. Arthur Clifford. (2 Vols. 1809.)

2. CONTEMPORARY AND SEVENTEENTH CENTURY WRITINGS.

Brantôme, Pierre de Bourdeille, Abbé de, *Book of the Ladies: Illustrious Dames.* (trans. Catherine Prescott Wormley. 1899.)

Buchanan, George. *History of Scotland.* (Anon. Trans. Edinburgh, 1752.)

Calderwood, David. *History of the Kirk of Scotland, 1524–1625.* (8 Vols. Wodrow Society. 1842–1849.)

Diurnal of Remarkable Occurrents, 1513–1575. Ed. Thomas Thomson. (Bannatyne and Maitland Clubs, 1833.)

Drummond, William, of Hawthornden. *History of Scotland.* (London, 1655.)

Knox, John, *History of the Reformation in Scotland.* (Wodrow Society, 3 Vols. 1846.)

Lesley, John, *History of Scotland, 1437–1561.* Ed. Thomas Thomson (Bannatyne Club, 1830.)

Lindsay, Sir David, of the Mount, *Works.* Ed. Douglas Hamer. (Scottish Text Society.)

Lindsay, Robert, of Pitscottie, *Historie and Cronicles of Scotland, 1437–1575.* Ed. Æneas J. G. Mackay. (3 Vols. Scottish Text Society. 1899–1911).

(Magdaleine). *Elegie Nuptiale Presentée à Madame Magdaleine, première Fille de France . . .* (Paris, 1537.)

Nicolay, Nicholas de, Seigneur d'Arfeuille, *La Navigation de Roy d'Ecosse Jacques cinquiesme du nom . . .* (1583) (also entitled *The Life and Death of King James the Fifth.* Miscellanea Scotica, 1818.)

Vergil, Polydore, *Anglica Historia, AD 1485–1537.* Ed. and trans. Denys Hay. (Camden Series LXXIV. Royal Historical Society. London 1950.)

Virelays Nuptiaux de Mariage du Roy d'Ecosse. Ed. Corde de Montaiglon (1855.)

3. NON-CONTEMPORARY BOOKS

Armstrong, W. A., *The Armstrong Borderland.* (North Berwick 1960.)

Bapst, 1, *Les Mariages de Jacques V.* (Paris, 1889.)

Barbé, Louis A., *In Byways of Scottish History.* (London, 1924.)

Bellsheim, A., *History of the Catholic Church in Scotland.* (trans. Hunter Blair. 4 Vols. Edinburgh. 1887–1890).

Bowle, John, *Henry VIII.* (London, 1964.)

Brown, P. Hume, *George Buchanan, Humanist and Reformer.* (Edinburgh, 1890.)

Brown, P. Hume, *History of Scotland*. (3 Vols. Cambridge, 1911.)

Chambers, Robert, *Biographical Dictionary of Eminent Scotsmen*. (Glasgow, 1835.)

Chapman, Hester. *The Sisters of Henry VIII*. (London, 1969.)

Chavrebière, Coissac de, *Histoire des Stuarts*. (Paris, 1930.)

Cook, E. Thornton. *Their Majesties of Scotland*. (London, 1930.)

Cruden, Stewart. *The Scottish Castle*. (Nelson, 1960.)

Dickinson, W. Croft, *Scotland from the Earliest Times to 1693*. (Nelson, 1961.)

Dickinson, W. Croft; Donaldson, Gordon; Milne, Isabel; *A Source Book of Scottish History*. (3 Vols. Nelson, 1953.)

Dictionary of National Biography.

Donaldson, Gordon, *The Reformation in Scotland*. (Cambridge, 1960.)

Donaldson, Gordon. *Scotland, James V to James VII*. (Oliver and Boyd, 1965.)

Donaldson, Gordon. *Scottish Kings*. (London, 1967.)

Duke, John A., *A History of the Church of Scotland to the Reformation*. (Edinburgh, 1957.)

Dunbar, Sir Archibald. H., *Scottish Kings*. (2nd edition. Edinburgh, 1906.)

Easson, D. E. *Gavin Dunbar, Chancellor of Scotland, Archbishop of Glasgow*. (Olwer and Boyd, 1947.)

Elder, Madge. *Ballad Country: the Scottish Border*. (Oliver and Boyd, 1963.)

Farmer, Henry George, *A History of Music in Scotland*. (London, 1947).

(François Ier). Le Duc de Lévis Mirepoix, Maurice Andrieux, Philippe Erlanger, Michel François, Jacques Levron, Pierre Mesnard, Régine Pernoud, Georges Poisson, *François Ier*, (Hachette, 1967).

Glover, Janet, *The Story of Scotland*. (London, 1960.)

Green, V. H. H. *Renaissance and Reformation: A Survey of European History between 1450 and 1660*. (2nd edition. London, 1964.)

Gregory, Donald. *History of the Western Highlands and Isles*. (2nd edition. London, 1881.)

Hackett, Francis, *Francis I*. (London, 1934.)

Hannay, Robert Kerr. *The College of Justice: Essays on the Institution and Development of the Court of Session*. (Edinburgh, 1933.)

Henderson, T. F., *The Royal Stewarts*. (Blackwood, 1914.)

Herkless, John, and Hannay, Robert Kerr, *The Archbishops of St Andrews*. (5 Vols. Edinburgh, 1907–1915.)

Herkless, John, *Cardinal Beaton, Priest and Politician*. (Edinburgh, 1891.)

Kinsley, James, *Scottish Poetry: a Critical Survey*. (London, 1955.)

Lang, Andrew, *History of Scotland*. (4 Vols. 3rd edition. Edinburgh, 1903–1907.)

Linklater, Eric. *The Royal House of Scotland*. (London, 1970.)

Mackenzie, Agnes Mure, *An Historical Survey of Scottish Literature to 1714*. (London, 1933.)

Mackenzie, Agnes Mure, *The Rise of the Stewarts*. (London, 1935.)

Mackenzie, Agnes Mure, *The Scotland of Queen Mary and the Religious Wars, 1513–1638*. (London, 1936.)

Mackenzie, W. C., *The Highlands and Isles of Scotland: A Historical Survey*. (revised edition. Edinburgh, 1949.)

Mackie, J. D., *The Earlier Tudors*. (2nd edition. Oxford, 1957.)

Mackie, J. D., *A History of Scotland*. (London, 1964.)

Maclean, Fitzroy. *A Concise History of Scotland*. (London, 1970.)

Masson, Rosaline. *Scotland the Nation*. (Nelson, 1934.)

Mitchison, Rosalind. *A History of Scotland*. (London, 1970.)

Nelson, William, *John Skelton, Laureate*. (Columbia University Press, 1939.)

Notestein, Wallace, *The Scot in History*. (London, 1946.)

Oliphant, Margaret, (Mrs Oliphant), *Royal Edinburgh*. (London, 1890.)

Oxford Book of Ballads. Ed. Sir A. Quiller-Couch. (1910.)

Oxford Book of Scottish Verse. Ed. John MacQueen and Tom Scott. (1966.)

Paul, Sir James Balfour, (Ed.) *The Scots Peerage*. (9 Vols. Edinburgh 1904–1914.)

Pinkerton, John *The History of Scotland, from the Accessions of the House of Stewart to that of Mary*. (2 Vols. 1797.)

Robertson, Iain Stuart, *An Introduction to the Poetry of Scotland, with a Guide to the Development of the Scottish Language*. (Forthcoming.)

Routh, C. R. N., *Who's Who in History, 1485–1603*. (Basil Blackwell, 1964.)

Scarisbrick, J. J. *Henry VIII*. (London, 1968.)

Stewart, I. H., *The Scottish Coinage*. (London, 1955.)

Strickland, Agnes, *The Queens of Scotland and English Princesses.* (8 Vols. Blackwood. 1850–1859.)

Stuart, Marie, W., *The Scot who was a Frenchman; being the Life of John Stewart, Duke of Albany, in Scotland, France and Italy.* (Hodge, 1940.)

Tytler, Patrick Fraser, *History of Scotland, 1249–1603.* (9 Vols. 2nd edition. Edinburgh, 1841–1843.)

Warrack, John, *Domestic Life in Scotland, 1488–1688.* (London, 1920.)

4. PAMPHLETS AND PUBLICATIONS IN PERIODICALS.

Collier, W. D., *The Scottish Regalia.* (HMSO Edinburgh, 1970.)

Dickinson, W. Croft, *The Scottish Reformation and Its Influence on Scottish Life and Character.* (Edinburgh, 1960.)

Donaldson, Gordon, (Ed.) *Common Errors in Scottish History.* (Historical Association Pamphlet. General Series No. G. 32.)

Dunbar, J. G.; Hay, G. D.; Quick, G. B., *The Stirling Heads.* (HMSO Edinburgh, 1960.)

Hannay, Robert Kerr, *The Scottish Crown and the Papacy 1424–1560.* (Historical Association of Scotland Pamphlets. New Series, No. 6.)

Mackie, J. D. *Henry VIII and Scotland.* (Transactions of the Royal Historical Society. 4th Series XXIX.)

Moncrieffe of that Ilk, Sir Iain. *The Royal Palace of Falkland.* (3rd Edition. Edinburgh. 1963.)

Murray, Atholl L., *Accounts of the King's Purse-Master, 1539–1540.* (Miscellany of the Scottish History Society. Vol. X. Edinburgh, 1965.)

Richardson, J. S., *The Abbey and Palace of Holyroodhouse.* (HMSO Edinburgh, 1950.)

Richardson, J. S., and Beveridge, James, *Linlithgow Palace.* (HMSO Edinburgh 1948.)

Richardson, J. S., and Root, Margaret E., *Stirling Castle.* (HMSO Edinburgh, 1948.)

Sinclair, Hon George A., *The Scots at Solway Moss.* (Scottish Historical Review. Vol. II. Glasgow, 1905.)

Index

Aberdeen, Bishop of (Gavin Dunbar), 49, 78

Albany, Alexander, Duke of, 23, 28, 30

Albany, John, Duke of, Regent, 28, 30, 31, 32, 33, 34, 35, 36, 37, 38, 39, 40, 41, 43, 44, 45, 46, 47, 48, 49, 51, 52, 53, 57, 58, 59, 60, 67, 68, 79, 80, 81, 100, 101, 103, 104, 114, 118, 139, 146, 168, 183

Alexander III, King of Scots, 14

Angus, 5th Earl of (Archibald Douglas, "Bell-the-Cat"), 19, 31, 184

Angus, 6th Earl of (Archibald Douglas), second husband of Margaret Tudor, 18, 31, 32, 33, 35, 36, 37, 38, 41, 42, 43, 44, 49, 51, 58, 59, 60, 61, 62, 63, 64, 65, 66, 67, 68, 69, 70, 71, 72, 73, 74, 75, 77, 78, 79, 80, 82, 83, 85, 86, 87, 88, 100, 102, 105, 129, 138, 139, 140, 141, 176, 181, 182

d'Arces, Antoine, Sieur de la Bastie, 40, 41

d'Arfeuille, see Nicholas de Nicolay

Argyll, 3rd Earl of (Colin Campbell), 49, 60, 62, 64, 74, 78, 80, 85

Argyll, 4th Earl of (Archibald Campbell), 85, 86, 87, 118, 129, 190, 194

Ariosto, Ludovico, 12

Armstrong, John, of Gilnockie ("Johnie Armstrong"), 83, 84, 85, 92, 148, 153

Armstrong, Thomas, of Mangerton, 85

Arran, 1st Earl of (James Hamilton), 31, 37, 38, 41, 42, 48, 49, 59, 60, 61, 62, 65, 74, 78, 118

Arran, 2nd Earl of (James Hamilton, later Duke of Châtelhérault), 118, 161, 162, 185, 193, 194, 195, 196

Arthur, Prince, second son of James V, 166, 177

Atholl, 3rd Earl of (John Stewart), 89, 90, 126

d'Auvergne, Agnès de la Tour, mother of Regent Albany, 30

d'Auvergne, Anne de la Tour, Comtesse, wife of Regent Albany, 30, 48, 101

Ayala, Pedro de, Spanish Ambassador to Scotland, 16, 24, 56

Barlow, William, Bishop-elect of St Asaph, emissary to Scotland, 110, 111

Barton, Sir Andrew, 79

Barton, Robert, 79

Beaton, David, Abbot of Arbroath, Archbishop of St Andrews, Cardinal, 79, 113, 134, 135, 146, 147, 154, 161, 162, 178, 179, 181, 184, 185, 189, 190, 194, 195, 196

Beaton, Elizabeth, of Criech, mistress of James V, 95

Beaton, James, Chancellor and Archbishop of Glasgow, Archbishop of St Andrews, 31, 49, 54, 62, 64, 65, 66, 78, 79, 107, 108, 112, 113, 146, 150, 155, 156

Bellenden, Thomas, 152

Blount, Elizabeth, mistress of Henry VIII, 137

Boece, Hector, scholar and historian, 20

Boleyn, Ann, second wife of Henry VIII, 110, 142

Boleyn, Mary, mistress of Henry VIII, 137

Borthwick, Lord, 36

Bothwell, 3rd Earl of (Patrick Hepburn), 74, 78, 87, 88

Bourbon, Cardinal de, 125

Bowes, Sir Robert, 181, 182

Brantôme, Pierre de Bourdeille, Abbé de, 123, 124, 130, 131

Brownhill, John, Master Mason, 169

Buccleuch, see Scott

Buchanan, George, historian and reformer, 12, 20, 70, 71, 76, 78, 81, 88, 94, 117, 132, 141, 150, 151

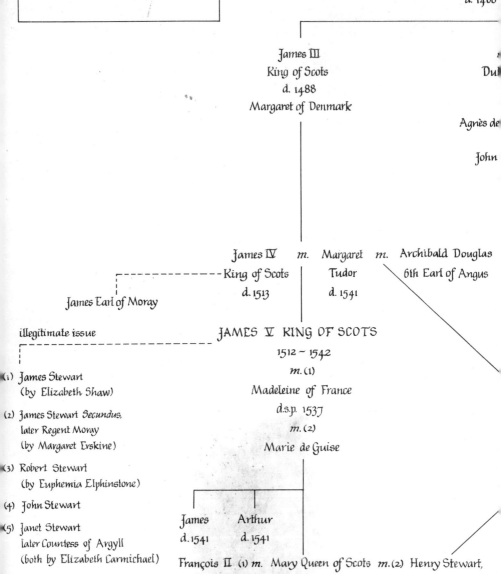

GENEALOGICAL TABLE

James II
King of Sc[...]
d. 1460

James III
King of Scots
d. 1488
Margaret of Denmark

Du[...]

Agnès de

John

James IV   *m.*   Margaret   *m.*   Archibald Douglas
King of Scots   Tudor   6th Earl of Angus
d. 1513   d. 1541

James Earl of Moray

illegitimate issue   JAMES V KING OF SCOTS

1512 ~ 1542

m. (1)

(1) James Stewart   Madeleine of France
(by Elizabeth Shaw)   d.s.p. 1537

(2) James Stewart *Secundus,*   *m.* (2)
later Regent Moray
(by Margaret Erskine)   Marie de Guise

(3) Robert Stewart
(by Euphemia Elphinstone)

(4) John Stewart

(5) Janet Stewart   James   Arthur
later Countess of Argyll   d. 1541   d. 1541
(both by Elizabeth Carmichael)

     François II (1) *m.* Mary Queen of Scots *m.* (2) Henry Stewart,
(6) Adam Stewart   of France   Lord Darnley
(by Elizabeth Stewart*)

(7) A Child, name and sex unknown   James VI of Scotland and I of E[...]
(by Elizabeth Beaton)

* *Elizabeth Stewart is often described as the daughter of
John, 3rd Earl of Lennox. He, however, had only one daughter,
who was named Helen. Elizabeth Stewart was possibly
one of the five daughters of John, 2nd Earl of Atholl.*